AND FAT FREDDY'S BLUES

A Comedy in Two Acts

by

P. J. BARRY

SAMUEL FRENCH, INC.

45 WEST 25TH STREET — NEW YORK 10010

7623 SUNSET BOULEVARD — HOLLYWOOD 90046

LONDON — *TORONTO*

ISBN 0 573 62652 9 Printed in the U.S.A.

IMPORTANT BILLING AND CREDIT REQUIREMENTS

All producers of AND FAT FREDDY'S BLUES *must* give credit to the Author of the Play in all programs distributed in connection with performances of the Play and in all instances in which the title of the Play appears for purposes of advertising, publicizing or otherwise exploiting the Play and/or a production. The name of the Author *must* also appear on a separate line, on which no other name appears, immediately following the title, and *must* appear in size of type not less than fifty percent the size of the title type.

AND FAT FREDDY'S BLUES premiered on June 7, 1996 at Stage West (Jerry Russell, Artistic Director; Diane Anglim, Executive Director) in Fort Worth, Texas. It was directed by P. J. Barry, with scenery and costumes by Jim Covault, lighting by Michael O'Brien, and stage management by Sondra Speer. The cast was as follows:

RUSS CALHOUN .... Peter Dobbins

DIANE CAPUTO.. Jennifer Hester

FAT FREDDY CAPUTO.................................. Jerry Russell

JEANNIE BROWN CALHOUN ....Deborah Sammons

Stage readings of **AND FAT FREDDY'S BLUES** have been presented by The Eugene O'Neill National Playwrights Conference, CT.; Shelykova Festival of New Plays, Russia (in Russian); ESIPA, Albany, NY; The York Theatre Co., NYC; and PKE Theatre, Los Angeles, CA.

AND FAT FREDDY'S BLUES

THE CHARACTERS

FAT FREDDY, 55. Once heavy, now much thinner.
RUSS, 29, rangy, handsome.
DIANE, 26, voluptuous. Fat Freddy's daughter.
JEANNIE, 22, pretty. Russ' wife.

The action of the play takes place in
Russ' bungalow in Jericho, Rhode Island.

ACT I

Scene 1 A February night, 1952. About 8 P.M.
Scene 2 Three days later. About midnight.
Scene 3 An hour later.

ACT II

Scene 1 Three days later. Afternoon.
Scene 2 The same day. Midnight.
Scene 3 Two days later. Late afternoon

THE SETTING:

The living room/dining area in a bungalow in the town of Jericho, Rhode Island.

It is well kept, comfortable, but cluttered—sofa with matching chair, overstuffed chair, floor lamp, end tables, table lamps, bookscase, a footstool, an ottoman, large rug and a fireplace. There are three caned chairs, a handmade dining room table and a credenza by the Upstage Right kitchen entrance. There are also three used attached theatre chairs by the center front door entrance. Downstage left there is an entrance into the bedroom and bathroom.

To

Ella Ellis

my longtime writer friend

ACT I

Scene 1

(A February night, 1952. About 8 P.M. Living room/dining area of RUSS' bungalow. At lights rise: RUSS, with a black eye, stands in the middle of the room. He is dejected. He moves to the telephone, starts to dial, hangs up, sits, lonely. Then he rises almost immediately, returns to the telephone, again starts to dial, then again hangs up. There is a knock at the door. RUSS brightens, moving quickly to open the door.)

RUSS. *(Opening the door.)* What the hell...?

DIANE. Surprised to see me?

RUSS. Yeah.

DIANE. *(Entering, wearing a short-skirted skating outfit, skates slung over her shoulder.)* Are we alone?

RUSS. Yeah.

(RUSS closes the door.)

DIANE. I came to apologize. I couldn't help myself... on the street... when I kissed you. I was possessed... by the devil. He made me do it... propelled me into your arms.

RUSS. Propelled?

DIANE. Of course. I didn't wreck your marriage. It was wrecked the day you married her. Where did the little wifey go? Back to Mommy and Daddy?

RUSS. How did you know we were separated?

DIANE. I have spies. Where'd you get the black eye?

RUSS. I ran into a door. What are you doing with skates?

DIANE. I'm going skating.

RUSS. Is this your wholesome night?

DIANE. It's a side of me you never got to explore.

RUSS. *(Refusing the bait.)* I just never knew you skated.

DIANE. Oh, I was a whiz in high school... couldn't keep me off the ice... or out of the woods. And tonight, on my way home, I was driving by Cobb's Pond and I saw the bonfire and the skaters and it looked good and when I got home I got these out of the basement, changed my clothes, and here I am, winter wonderland, at your doorstep. Want to come with me?

RUSS. Let me get this straight. You came here to apologize for kissing me in the street last—

DIANE. *Was* the breakup my fault?

RUSS. It had nothing to do with—

DIANE. It did. I kissed you *passionately* in front of her, you know it—

RUSS. I told her you were impulsive and a little nuts. She accepted that.

DIANE. You're lying. I am the cause.

RUSS. No, Diane.

DIANE. *(Removing skates from around her shoulder.)* Then what? Ahhhhh. You want it every night. She's timid... once-a-week... in-the-dark. Oh, Russ... poor horney baby.

RUSS. You'd better go skating.

DIANE. I need to warm up for a minute. It's cold out there.

Like my outfit?

(And DIANE twirls.)

RUSS. *(Pause.)* Yeah...
DIANE. It shows off my legs.
RUSS. I know.
DIANE. I have good legs.
RUSS. I know.
DIANE. You always said.
RUSS. I know.
DIANE. Hi.
RUSS. Diane—
DIANE. Like my earmuffs, too? —You gave them to me. Remember?
RUSS. I don't remember.
DIANE. Two Christmases ago, on—
RUSS. I don't remem—
DIANE. You do. On Christmas Eve. In front of the fire? I wore just the earmuffs. *(RUSS smiles.)* You remember. *(He lets his guard down. They share a quiet laugh.)* How could you forget.
RUSS. You're warm enough now.

(RUSS heads toward the door.)

DIANE. Wait. I brought you a Valentine present, something inexpensive, I didn't go overboard. I couldn't resist. *(From a pocket she removes an aluminum-foiled chocolate heart.)* A token of my affection. *(Crosses to him, offers it, he accepts.)* Happy Valentine's Day. *(Knowing it's dangerous close to her, he moves away.)* Don't I get a thank you. *(No response.)* "Thank you." You're welcome. Will you be my Valentine?

RUSS. No.

DIANE. Grouch. *(Pause.)* Can I have a piece... of your chocolate heart? *(RUSS removes the aluminum foil, and offers it to her. She goes to him and breaks off a piece of chocolate.)* Thank you. *(Pause.)* "You're welcome."

RUSS. *(Again moving away from her. Halfheartedly.)* Diane, get the earmuffs back on, pick up your skates and—

DIANE. Come with me. We'll have fun. Come with me, please.

RUSS. No. Diane, I'm a married man.

DIANE. Waiting for the little wifey to return?

RUSS. Yes... No. She took all her clothes.

DIANE. Oh, good.

RUSS. But she'll be back. We both need a little time, that's all.

DIANE. She took all her clothes... that doesn't sound—

RUSS. Things have a way of working themselves out.

DIANE. It'll never work out. She's a drip.

RUSS. *She's not a drip,* she's just... sincere.

DIANE. Exactly, a sincere drip.

RUSS. *(Riled.)* Shut up, Diane! No more names, okay?— *Just shut up!*

DIANE. *(Miffed.)* You know... I take a lot from you that I wouldn't take from anybody else because I still... care about you. *(RUSS grunts.)* It's true.

RUSS. You broke it off... to marry that lawyer moneybags from—

DIANE. But I didn't! That was my father's stupid idea, and I... I couldn't jump into another marriage with him or you or anybody. I was not... using my head.

RUSS. Hey. You dumped, me, I wasn't good enough for you.

DIANE. I miss you.

RUSS. Geezuz.

DIANE. I love you.

RUSS. Sure.

DIANE. I do.

RUSS. Because I'm married to somebody else.

DIANE. *(Miffed again.)* Wait a minute, *just-one-minute*, you. *(Pause.)* You've been married seven months... and this is the first conversation we've had... except last week on the street when I kissed you and offered my belated congratulations.

RUSS. *(Overlapping.)* You offered trouble.

DIANE. I didn't go near the Majestic, I avoided you, I didn't invade your privacy, I wasn't becoming the local homewrecker.

RUSS. So what are you doing here tonight?

DIANE. You're separated. That's different.

RUSS. You just knock on the door, and expect—

DIANE. You want me to be humble?

RUSS. It would kill you.

DIANE. *(Humbly/Sincerely.)* I was a fool. I was wrong, I'm lonely, I do miss you, I can't live without you. *(Pause.)* I love you, I always will.

RUSS. *(Pause.)* Go skating, go on... before everybody's gone, before the bonfire goes out... Geezuz. Coming to apologize—What a fraud! Did you think if you came bouncing in here I'd hop into bed with you?

DIANE. I brought you a chocolate heart.

RUSS. You walked out of my life, I got married, you can't walk back in.

DIANE. Of course I can. I walked back in. I'm here.

RUSS. You drive me crazy!

DIANE. The feeling is mutual. How do we reconcile our differences?

(No response. Impasse. RUSS lights a cigarette, then sits in one of the theatre chairs. He glances at DIANE, she smiles, he turns away. She hesitates, then quickly sits in a theatre chair, leaving an empty one between them.)

DIANE. *(Referring to the three attached theatre chairs.)* From the Majestic?

RUSS. *(Nods.)* The put new chairs in the balcony last month. They were gonna throw out the old ones. I took these three.

DIANE. What a bargain.

RUSS. It's where we met... Jeannie and me... in the balcony. It was the last show. *A Streetcar Named Desire.* The lights came up. I came out of the booth. She was alone... sitting in this seat. She was crying...

DIANE. And you comforted her.

RUSS. That's how we met, that's how we fell in love.

DIANE. So you met a weeper in the balcony and married her—Whoopee.

RUSS. Look, she's sincere and sweet and sexy and—

DIANE. Sexy!

(DIANE laughs.)

RUSS. Yeah, in her way.

DIANE. *(Overlapping.)* Oh, Russ, oh, Russ, poor baby, you—

RUSS. *(Annoyed.)* What do you know?

DIANE. I understand. You were on the rebound, you made a mistake, admit it. You've missed me, too, I can feel—

RUSS. You don't listen, do—

DIANE. The solution is simple, you know. Get a divorce.

RUSS. I can't, I'm a Catholic.

DIANE. Since when have you been a stickler for—

RUSS. I've changed.

DIANE. You don't even believe in God.

RUSS. I've done an about face.

DIANE. No, you haven't—All right, don't get a divorce. There are ways around it. My marriage was annulled.

RUSS. Sure. Your father bribed the Bishop.

DIANE. How do you know that?

RUSS. You told me.

DIANE. I told you that?

RUSS. Yeah.

DIANE. When?

RUSS. We were in the bathtub.

DIANE. Whose?

RUSS. Yours.

DIANE. I don't remember telling you that. Why would I tell you that in the bathtub?

RUSS. I've never tried to figure you out.

DIANE. Well, keep it to yourself. My father hates it when I blab family secrets—Well, maybe not so much anymore.

RUSS. How is Fat Freddy?

DIANE. Getting thinner. He goes back into the hospital on Friday.

RUSS. Another operation?

DIANE. *(Nods.)* Dr. Russo *sounds* hopeful. No matter, Fat

Freddy'll pull through... again.

RUSS. His kind always do. *(Pause.)* Crooks.

DIANE. *(Giving him a friendly swat.)* He's not a crook... anymore. That was the old days.

RUSS. His daughter took over and made him legitimate.

DIANE. That's the rumor. Can I have another piece of your heart?

RUSS. *(Pointing to the table.)* Help yourself.

DIANE. *(Moves into chair beside him.)* You are glad to see me.

RUSS. *(Not moving.)* Geezuz.

DIANE. You are. *(Pause.)* What? *(Pause.)* I'm not sleeping with anybody.

RUSS. Who asked?

DIANE. I've been faithful to you. Well, almost. There was only one.

RUSS. *(Rises, moving away from her.)* I don't want to hear.

DIANE. A lieutenant going overseas... to Korea.

RUSS. *(Putting out the cigarette.)* Doing your part for the war effort?

DIANE. Exactly. He was... so lonely... it was Thanksgiving! One day... well, one night... well, Thanksgiving weekend, what the hell. I was... giving... on Thanksgiv—

RUSS. I got it.

DIANE. I'm being honest. I'm human. Forgive me?

RUSS. *(Riled.)* Forgive you for what? You act like you're my wife and Jeannie's the other woman!

DIANE. She is. I had you first.

RUSS. You'd better leave.

DIANE. Did she give you the black eye? How did she do it? A frying pan?

RUSS. Her brother gave me the—

DIANE. Her brother?! You mean it was a family—

RUSS. Our differences had nothing to do with you... Is that clear? Maybe it'll take a little time, but we'll work it out and she'll be back.

DIANE. You want her back?

RUSS. Diane, I'm trying to keep my marriage going!

DIANE. Why? She's a drip!

RUSS. Cut out the name calling!

DIANE. You can't stay married to that—She'll drive you insane.

RUSS. You're wrong. She *brings* me sanity.

DIANE. She'll bring you crying babies, that's what she'll bring. Are you ready for that? Support a bunch of crying—

RUSS. Maybe they won't cry.

DIANE. All babies cry.

RUSS. Do you want a beer?—No, you don't. I do, you don't. Go skating, goodnight.

(RUSS exits into the kitchen.)

DIANE. *(Taken aback.)* You want me to go?

RUSS. *(From offstage.)* Yeah.

DIANE. No you don't.

RUSS. I do!

DIANE. You *really* want me to—

RUSS. I WANT YOU TO GO! GO!

(Angry, DIANE starts toward the door. RUSS returns with a can of beer.)

RUSS. Don't forget your skates.

DIANE. *(Grabbing up the skates.)* You think you can ignore me?!

RUSS. GET OUT!

DIANE. *(Pause.)* I hope your dick falls off.

(DIANE exits.)

RUSS. *(Shouting.)* No you don't!

(Door swings open. DIANE is back. She closes the door.)

DIANE. *(With restraint.)* All right. I made a mistake. You made a mistake. Let's start all over again.

RUSS. *(With restraint.)* Diane. Please. Go skating.

(DIANE is about to respond, changes her mind, and storms out, slamming the door after her.)

(BLACKOUT)

(Music.)

Scene 2

(Three days later. Midnight. As lights rise: FAT FREDDY, in his overcoat, sits comfortably in an overstuffed armchair. A briefcase is set alongside the chair. His hat is on the table.

RUSS enters from outside, startled to see him.)

RUSS. What are you doing in my house?

FAT FREDDY. President Truman sent me. He wants you to re-enlist. Got a secret mission for you in Korea.

RUSS. *(Pause.)* You just walk in and make yourself at home?

FAT FREDDY. The door was unlocked. An unlocked door means you're a trusting man.

RUSS. Not in the dead of night.

FAT FREDDY. It's midnight. Three A.M. is the dead of night, three A.M. people are lookin' for trouble, but midnight?... naw... discussion's still possible. Come on in, you live here.

RUSS. Mr. Caputo...

FAT FREDDY. No, no... nobody calls me Mr. Caputo. I'm Fat Freddy to my family, my friends, my enemies... even the Governor. 'Course, I ain't the size I used to be. People say: "'Scuse me, but why they call ya Fat Freddy, 'scuse me for askin'," people ask like that. I don't explain—Shut the door—I tell 'em I'm goin' back into the hospital, they don't wanna hear. Shut the door, you're wastin' good fuel. *(RUSS shuts the door.)* That's better. Chilly out there. Not so warm in here either when I come in... I raised the thermostat, you can tell. Surprised ya got an oil burner in this shack. That's some shiner. What happened?

RUSS. I ran into a door.

(RUSS removes his jacket.)

FAT FREDDY. How was the movie business tonight?

RUSS. Pretty good. Jimmy Stewart still packs 'em in.

FAT FREDDY. Never liked that skinny jerk. *(Imitates him.)* "Well, well, well..." I like 'em with some punch... like Jimmy Cagney. Jimmy Stewart, no, Jimmy Cagney, yes. You agree?

RUSS. No.

FAT FREDDY. *(Pause.)* You like your job? You like bein' a projectionist?

RUSS. It pays the bills.

FAT FREDDY. How long you worked at the Majestic?

RUSS. *(Pause.)* A little over a year.

FAT FREDDY. And before that?

RUSS. Is this gonna be twenty questions or what?

FAT FREDDY. Before that, before you went to work at the Majestic, you was drivin' for Jericho Cabs and when I bought 'em out you wouldn't come drive for me. Why?

RUSS. None of your business.

FAT FREDDY. You gettin' smart with me?

RUSS. You're in my house, uninvited, I can get smart with you.

FAT FREDDY. And way before that, after you got all them medals for fighting the Japs, after the war, you was in that Veteran's hospital for somethin' like twenty months, shot up bad, and they finally patch you back together—ya body, ya brain—and you come out and get hired and fired, flip-flop jobs, gettin' in fights over nothin'... until you start drivin' cab, and you lasted, got ya feet back on the ground again. I know everything about you...

RUSS. They why ask questions if you know the answers.

FAT FREDDY. *(Ignoring his remark.)* So, like I said, I offered you a chance after I bought out Jericho Cabs to come drive for me and you said no *because*—

RUSS. Because I was involved with your daughter at the

time—I didn't like mixing business with pleasure—but I haven't been involved with your daughter... must be over a year. You are here about your daughter, am I right? I'm right.

FAT FREDDY. Why ask questions if ya got the answers. I'm thirsty. Whatya got?

RUSS. Want a beer?

FAT FREDDY. Beer's fine.

RUSS. I've only got cans. You want a glass with it?

FAT FREDDY. Can's fine. *(RUSS exits.)* Know how you got your job at the Majestic?

RUSS. *(Offstage.)* Yeah.

FAT FREDDY. You do?

RUSS. Yeah.

FAT FREDDY. Diane came to me, told me you wouldn't come drive cab for us so she asks me to pull a few strings and I did and you got that job.

RUSS. *(Returning with beers.)* No. A Dr. Greenberg at the Vet's Hospital got me the job through his brother-in-law who owns the Majestic.

FAT FREDDY. That's what you think.

RUSS. That's what I know.

FAT FREDDY. You callin' me a liar?

RUSS. *(Pause.)* Yeah.

FAT FREDDY. Nobody calls me a liar.

RUSS. I just did.

FAT FREDDY. You better stay alert.

RUSS. *(Opening beers with a church key.)* Should I worry about you pulling out a gun and shooting me?

FAT FREDDY. You see too many movies.

RUSS. I see them everyday.

FAT FREDDY. Yeah. *(Pause.)* About that. Must be I called

Harvey Schulman at the Majestic—he owed me a favor—'bout the same time his brother-in-law, your Dr. Greenberg called 'im. I'd say *both of us* was... instrumental in gettin' you that projectionist job.

RUSS. *(Pause.)* That's possible.

(RUSS offers a beer.)

FAT FREDDY. Thanks.

RUSS. You're welcome.

FAT FREDDY. How long have you been married?

RUSS. You don't know?

FAT FREDDY. Seven months. How's it been? Not so good?

RUSS. You're here to talk about your daughter.

FAT FREDDY. I'll get there. Gotta clean up a few things first along the way.

RUSS. Like my marriage?

FAT FREDDY. Right now you're separated. The wife went home to her folks. Not so good... not good at all. So how much you want to get a divorce.

RUSS. *(Pause.)* You go fast.

FAT FREDDY. Speak.

RUSS. I can't. It's against the church.

FAT FREDDY. We can work around that. How much?

RUSS. I love my wife.

FAT FREDDY. She's got no tits.

RUSS. *Hey.*

FAT FREDDY. I've seen her in the bank—I insulted your wife... how come you're not defendin' her?

RUSS. I should punch you in the face?

FAT FREDDY. If you loved her, you'd defend her.

RUSS. You're a man in poor health... going back into the hospital... I hear you might not make it this time around.

FAT FREDDY. Is that what you hear.

RUSS. I take pity on a man who might—

FAT FREDDY. Who might have a gun and blow your head off?

RUSS. You do have a gun.

FAT FREDDY. I'm full of surprises. You love you wife you say?

RUSS. I just told you.

FAT FREDDY. You love my daughter?

RUSS. *(Pause.)* I did.

FAT FREDDY. You did, but you don't anymore?

RUSS. *I said I did.*

FAT FREDDY. You still love her?

RUSS. No.

FAT FREDDY. I'm smart. You do.

RUSS. Maybe

FAT FREDDY. You do.

RUSS. So what if I do?

FAT FREDDY. So you love two women at once.

RUSS. So what? I live with one, I don't live with the other. Makes a difference.

FAT FREDDY. *(Overlapping.)* Right now you not *living* with anybody.

RUSS. Right now that's okay.

FAT FREDDY. But you admit you love my daughter, too.

RUSS. You can love somebody... and not see them.

FAT FREDDY. You saw her the other night. She dropped by here, wanted ya to go skatin'.

RUSS. Yeah.

FAT FREDDY. *(Overlapping.)* Wound up skatin' by herself. You're no gentleman.

RUSS. I'm no puppet.

FAT FREDDY. She loves you, too. She told me... usually keeps things to herself... you know... I caught her cryin'. Ain't seen her cryin' like that since she was a kid. And when I croak... she gets it all, she'll be richer than rich. The real estate office, the truckin' company, the cab company, the—

RUSS. I know what you own.

FAT FREDDY. She runs everything for me now... What a head for figures... and she's a fireball. Her only drawback is men.

RUSS. Look—

FAT FREDDY. *(Overlapping.)* Granted, that first marriage, I sorta arranged it. I thought the guy was aces, turned out to be a saphead. 'Course, she was just a kid then... so I got her unattached fast.

RUSS. I heard.

(RUSS lights a cigarette.)

FAT FREDDY. But she still needed her lovin'... got that from me, not her mother... her mother was a dud. I knew she'd taken up with you when you was drivin' for Jericho Cabs. A screwed up war hero's better than some saphead, but—

RUSS. Thanks.

FAT FREDDY. Don't get me wrong, I respect veterans, but... you are who you are.

RUSS. A screwed up war hero—

FAT FREDDY. Exactly, so I did a little arrangin' again, old friend's son, bigshot lawyer, and she *almost* bit...

RUSS. Did she.

FAT FREDDY. ... 'cause I don't want her marryin' you, can't... what are you? A cab driver.

RUSS. A screwed up cab driver.

FAT FREDDY. Exactly. I told her she's on her way up... why get attached... to a bump-on-a-log?

RUSS. Thanks again.

FAT FREDDY. *(Overlapping.)* But now... change! You're a projectionist, half-a-step-up from a bump-on-a-log. You're makin' progress.

RUSS. That's good to know.

FAT FREDDY. She says you *were* the one for her... she let ya go 'cause I told her ya got no ambition.

RUSS. But now I'm half-a-step-up.

FAT FREDDY. That's what I said—Congratulations! She wants you, I'm here to see she gets you. *(RUSS laughs.)* This ain't a joke, sonny. In the mornin' I go back into the hospital and I'm takin' precautions... gettin' my house and my daughter in order.

RUSS. Mr. Caputo—

FAT FREDDY. Fat Freddy, sonny.

RUSS. Mr. Caputo, you don't seem to—

FAT FREDDY. Yes, I do. We'll get you divorced, have no fear. So tell me what you want, what's your price?

RUSS. None.

FAT FREDDY. You got a price, sonny.

RUSS. *(Pause.)* No deal.

FAT FREDDY. Ya wanna move up in the world, climb the ladder of success... ya don't stay cooped up in a projectionist booth.

RUSS. Gives me time to think about other things.

FAT FREDDY. Like what? Sex?

RUSS. No. Life.

FAT FREDDY. Hey. You don't think about life, sonny, you live it. I know. I have. Now. I'm here to keep my daughter happy, that's my concern, I want you to make it your concern. So. I'll set you up in business... buy out the theatres in Jericho... the Majestic *and* the Odeon. Harvey Schulman owns both of 'em, ya know, and he owes me some big favors so he'll sell 'em if I pressure enough. You can run both of 'em. The Majestic, the Odeon. Yours. How's that sound?

RUSS. Not real.

FAT FREDDY. You can rename one of 'em... like change the Majestic to the Calhoun Theatre. Sound classy?

RUSS. No.

FAT FREDDY. *Don't* change the name then.

RUSS. *(Overlapping.)* Mr. Caputo—

FAT FREDDY. How 'bout real estate? Change it from Caputo Real Estate to Caputo and Calhoun Real—

RUSS. No.

FAT FREDDY. Caputo and Calhoun Trucking Company?

RUSS. No.

FAT FREDDY. You're hard to please, sonny.

RUSS. From your corner, Mr. Caputo.

FAT FREDDY. You quit callin' me Mr. Caputo, I'll quit callin' you sonny. *(Pause.)* Okay. *(Reaches down, grabs up the briefcase beside him, and sets it on his lap.)* How about... half a million bucks in cash? *(Opens the briefcase.)* There. Five hundred thousand. Half a million bucks. *(Pause.)* Come over here. *(RUSS hesitates, then crosses to him. Pause.)* Ever seen that much money?

RUSS. No.

FAT FREDDY. *(Pause.)* You want it?

RUSS. *(Pause.)* Tempting.

FAT FREDDY. *(Laughs.)* You bet it is. *(Laughs again.)* Gets the blood flowin' fast, huh? *(Pause.)* Tempting, huh?

RUSS. Oh, yeah.

FAT FREDDY. *(Echoing him.)* Oh, yeah. *(Laughs again.)* Money's power... don't let anybody kid ya it ain't... 'cause it is. Power. Right here. Right in my lap.

RUSS. Is this money you made profiteering from the war while I was getting my ass shot off?

FAT FREDDY. Naw... not this money. This is clean. Fifteen years old. *(Pause.)* Ya finished lookin'?

RUSS. Yeah.

FAT FREDDY. My pleasure. *(Closes briefcase, puts it down.)* Ya don't need to make a decision right now. Just wanted to let you know I wasn't bluffin'.

RUSS. Look. I could take your money, take your daughter, and then... after you depart for places unknown... I could just take off.

FAT FREDDY. *(Aroused.)* I ain't departin' nowhere... *yet.* And when I make a deal with somebody, they don't renege. Know why? 'Cause I got friends owe me... outta the grave... in the grave.

RUSS. *(Pause.)* You come prepared.

FAT FREDDY. *(Calmly again.)* Always come prepared, always have a coupla *rearrangements* ready. Gotta have rearrangements or you can keel right over... fall off a roof... drown in cowshit... who knows? Coupla my old pals got their heads blown off 'cause they had no *rearrangements.* You take your time makin' up your mind... a few days'll be fine.

RUSS. Thanks for all the offers, but I'm not interested.

FAT FREDDY. *(Pause.)* You're an independent man.

RUSS. For the moment.

FAT FREDDY. *(Laughs.)* That's sensible thinkin'. Got a job today, could be gone tomorrow, right?

RUSS. It could.

FAT FREDDY. If you lost your job what would you do?

RUSS. There are other jobs.

FAT FREDDY. Like what?

RUSS. Carpentry... I'm getting pretty good at it.

FAT FREDDY. Oh, yeah... ?

RUSS. And there are other theatres... in other towns. *(FAT FREDDY sneezes.)* God bless you. *(FAT FREDDY sneezes again.)* God bless you.

FAT FREDDY. Thanks. *(Blows his nose.)* I need all the blessings I can get. Am I gettin' a cold? Am I, God? *(Confidentially. To RUSS.)* At this time in my life I'm keepin' communications open... right, God? *(Pause.)* Sonofabitch never answers. *(To above.)* Sorry. *(Pause.)* Listen. One thing. Diane doesn't know I was comin' here, I don't want her to know. Ya got me, Russ?

RUSS. I gotcha, Fat Freddy.

FAT FREDDY. *(Laughs.)* Okay. *(Pause.)* Okay. *(Pause.)* I'll be talkin' to you after I get outta the hospital. Or I'll give you a call from there, we'll get it settled. *(Attempts to rise, is having a little trouble.)* I don't like this... feelin' like an old man.

RUSS. You need a hand?

FAT FREDDY. No. *(Up on his feet now, straightens up.)* Last time I was in the hospital they took a growth outta me the size of a grapefruit. This time probably a watermelon. I asked the doc point blank. "Doc, I want the truth. Will I make it this time?" *(Pause.)* Some questions ya don't ask. *(Has a final slug of beer, sets it down.)* Ahhh... good beer. Always useta like beer with porkchops. Beer's the only thing compliments porkchops, ya know that? Beer, not wine. Porkchops was my favorite. But I still loved roast beef, pot roast... ravioli, lasagna, manicotti... mmmm... *(Pause.)* ... spare ribs, leg-a-lamb, veal parmesan, oh, yeah... ohhh, could I put it away. My housekeeper, Celia Chesniak, boy what a cook! But this last year... the appetite... ppppt!... out the window. And now I got restrictions. Now it's jello... oatmeal... custard... *(Pause.)* Pathetic. *(Pause.)* Tell ya somethin'. I usually preferred food to sex. That's the truth. You?

RUSS. I like a good meal.

FAT FREDDY. Sorry I asked. *(In reference to the table.)* You make this?

RUSS. The table, yeah... not the chairs.

FAT FREDDY. *(Appreciative.)* That's good work.

RUSS. Thanks.

FAT FREDDY. Damn good work. Carpentry business?

RUSS. Just a hobby. Keeps me out of trouble.

FAT FREDDY. Home made furnishings store? Set you up in—

RUSS. I told you, I got a job.

FAT FREDDY. No future runnin' movies on a screen. Where does that lead?

RUSS. *(Picks up the briefcase, gives it to FAT FREDDY.)* It got me a few unexpected offers tonight.

FAT FREDDY. Yeah...

RUSS. I don't think I made myself clear. I like my job. People like the movies, they like the happy endings.

FAT FREDDY. And you? You like lookin' at 'em, too? Don't ya see what I'm sayin'? Ya don't wanna do that for the rest of your life. I'm offerin' ya—

RUSS. Whatever the rest of my life turns out to be... I'll find it... my own way.

FAT FREDDY. You'll find it *my* way. You better wise up and do what I—

RUSS. *(Riled.)* Mr. Caputo, I had enough orders in the army, in the hospital. That's all over. It's my turn, *my way now...* a little peace and quiet.

FAT FREDDY. Peace and quiet. That's for old farts.

RUSS. I discovered that's what I want.

FAT FREDDY. You were with my daughter. Peace and—

RUSS. After your daughter, *after*. You were leaving. *Goodnight*, Mr. Caputo.

(RUSS hands FAT FREDDY his hat.)

FAT FREDDY. *(Tensing.)* Hey. I don't take no for an answer if that's the answer I don't wanna hear.

RUSS. *Who the hell do you think you are*?

FAT FREDDY. Watch it, sonny.

RUSS. You can't force people to do what they don't want to do.

FAT FREDDY. Sure I can. I've done it all my life.

RUSS. Yeah, and look. Your forced your daughter to marry some... some—

FAT FREDDY. Saphead.

RUSS. —saphead... and here you are trying to rectify what happened—

FAT FREDDY. If I want to *rectify*, I'll *rectify*!... the past, the future, whatever!... 'cause I ain't got long to get my daughter on her right track before I gotta... gotta face my Maker, and when I do, when I'm facin' God—eyeball to eyeball—you can be damn sure I'm gonna have a clean slate! *(Calming down. Firmly.)* I love my daughter more than anything in this world. She's gonna have what she wants. *(Takes out a gun, doesn't point it at him.)* You were right. I mean if you're carryin' this much money around ya gotta make sure ya got your own protection. *(Pause.)* So think it over. Use your head. Or somebody could blow your head off.

RUSS. Are you threatening me?

FAT FREDDY. Fat Freddy never threatens anybody. Never had to. *(Puts gun away.)* Like I said, alive or dead... I got a lotta friends owe me. Talk to you soon, Russ. *(And with his free hand gives him a very slight tap of a slap on the cheek.)* Remember. *(Pause.)* Rearrangements.

(FAT FREDDY exits. Silence. RUSS seethes. Then he goes to the telephone, dials.)

RUSS. Hello... Diane, your father is walking around with half a million dollars and a gun... Yeah, here... Get him a cage... *(JEANNIE appears in the bedroom doorway. She wears a jacket and carries a shoulder bag.)* On his way home, I guess... How the hell do I know?... It's not my problem, Diane... Yeah, bye.

JEANNIE. *(Upset.)* You should call the police, not *her.*

RUSS. *(Startled.)* Geezuz. Where did you... ?

JEANNIE. He was threatening you.

RUSS. You heard—

JEANNIE. I heard everything.

RUSS. You've been in the bedroom all—

JEANNIE. I heard *everything.*

RUSS. You're back.

JEANNIE. No, I'm not back, I just came to talk. I lay down on the bed... I fell asleep. I was waiting for you to get home... to *talk*... and I woke up hearing voices and—

RUSS. Oh, boy...

JEANNIE. Yes, *I-heard-everything.*

RUSS. You should've come out of there, instead of—

JEANNIE. I'm not back, don't think I am, I'm *not*... how could I now? I came to get my earrings... I forgot them, I had to borrow my mother's... I don't like hers, they're old fashioned. And I came to apologize for my brother. I found out that Arthur punched you outside the Majestic because you punched Dad that awful night here. I didn't ask Arthur to do that, I want you to know that... he left this morning, yes, he did enlist, and *yes,* we're proud of him. While I was here I intended to talk about the fight here that awful night. I thought if you apologized to my Dad for hitting him, maybe we could somehow manage to straighten out our situation but now when I heard what I heard—That man, that Fat Freddy is crazy—

RUSS. Sit down, Jeannie.

JEANNIE. *(Overlapping.)* —Walking around with half a million dollars *and* a gun... is that normal? No. And he threatened you. You should call the police... instead, you call *her.*

RUSS. Why don't you sit down?

JEANNIE. After what I heard?

RUSS. Jeannie—

JEANNIE. *(Overlapping.)* I don't believe what I heard. But then I was here that awful night when my father tried to reason with—

RUSS. *(Annoyed.)* Your father came in here swinging, calling *me* a traitor, calling me—

JEANNIE. Because you told Arthur not to enlist, you told Arthur to be a conscientious objector, you—

RUSS. Yeah, because war is shit, war is a waste—

JEANNIE. And then what did you do?

RUSS. Jeannie, World War II ended *only* seven years ago and—

JEANNIE. *What did you do*?

RUSS. —here we are, in Korea, up to our necks—

JEANNIE. You knocked my father out cold.

RUSS. I was defending myself.

JEANNIE. *(Overlapping.)* And then you smashed up half this room—

RUSS. I only smashed a chair.

JEANNIE. —And I didn't know who I was living with... and I come here tonight to... to make peace... to try, at least tell you to go see that Dr. Greenberg at the Vet's Hospital, that doctor you said you liked so much who helped you to become a civilian again, I came to *try*, and what happens? I hear you say to him... that crook, that crazy man, that father of *her*... I hear you say you love *her*.

RUSS. I said I l*oved* her.

JEANNIE. You said *then*... you said *now*. *(Restraining tears.)* Ohhhh, how I wish that Arthur had really hurt you, not given you just a black eye, but a broken nose, *yes*! I wish I had the strength to sock you because I would hurt you the way you hurt me... your wife... 'til death do us part, isn't that a joke... and do you know something? I'm speechless.

(JEANNIE sits. Silence.)

RUSS. *(Pause.)* You got a new jacket.

JEANNIE. It was on sale.

RUSS. You look good in that color.

JEANNIE. Everybody says that.

RUSS. Uh huh.

JEANNIE. You don't think it's too loud?

RUSS. Looks good, Jeannie. *(Pause.)* Take your jacket off. Here... let me take—

JEANNIE. No. *(Rising, defensive again, but still vulnerable.)* He asks you if you love me and you say yes and he asks you if you love her and you say no and then you change your mind and say yes, and I'm lying on the bed and I stuck the bedspread into my mouth so I wouldn't scream... and then to hear that she came here... and slept in my bed, don't deny it because I know—

RUSS. No, you don't *know.* She came her to go skating, that was it, she didn't get into any bed—Geezuz—you heard what he—

JEANNIE. His daughter wants you, *that's* what I heard. Talks about his own daughter like she's a whore—She is!—but a father shouldn't talk about his own daughter that way. He said you can make her happy if I'm not in the picture. Well, I *am* in the picture.

RUSS. You're not living here... how are you in the picture?

JEANNIE. *(Overlapping.)* I'm still your wife.

RUSS. You're not acting like a wife.

JEANNIE. How can I? You hurt me. *(Again on the verge of tears.)* I'm a hurt person.

RUSS. *(Pause.)* Did I accept his offers?

JEANNIE. *(Pause.)* No...

RUSS. Doesn't that prove something? *(Pause.)* Doesn't that

show you that I care about you? That I love you?

JEANNIE. *(Letting her guard down.)* Will he take away your job? Can he do that?

RUSS. I don't know.

JEANNIE. He can.

RUSS. I'm not worried, Jeannie.

JEANNIE. Was it really a half a million dollars in cash?

RUSS. I didn't get a chance to count it.

JEANNIE. I've counted that much in the bank. Like counting play money... like Monopoly money. Who walks around with half a million dollars?

RUSS. Fat Freddy. Sit down, honey.

JEANNIE. *(Defensive again.)* Don't call me honey. I'm going home.

RUSS. This is your home.

JEANNIE. No, it's not. *She's* been in it, she's been here... in *there*... she's—

RUSS. I told you, she was *not in*—

JEANNIE. I don't care, she's still a slut.

RUSS. Don't call her that.

JEANNIE. You see? You defend her but you don't defend me. You didn't when he talked about my... upper torso

RUSS. Your breasts.

JEANNIE. Yes, my... breasts. A lot you care.

RUSS. I've enjoyed them.

JEANNIE. They're small.

RUSS. They're beautiful.

JEANNIE. *(Less defensive.)* If you loved me you would've punched him when he insulted me.

(JEANNIE sits.)

RUSS. There's been enough punching around here.

JEANNIE. *(Overlapping.)* You didn't—

RUSS. Jeannie, the man is sick, probably dying. He goes back into the hospital in—

JEANNIE. You didn't defend me, I know that.

RUSS. *(Overlapping.)* Will you be reasonable?

JEANNIE. I—

RUSS. Stop. *(Crosses to her, kneels down in front of her.)* Be reasonable?

JEANNIE. *(Pause.)* I am... usually... aren't I? Is that what you meant by peace and quiet? Reasonable?

RUSS. No, honey.

JEANNIE. "*After her*" you said. Who wants to be known as peace and quiet?

RUSS. Nobody.

JEANNIE. Well, I'm not.

RUSS. Of course you're not.

JEANNIE. I'm me.

RUSS. Sure you are.

JEANNIE. Who am I?

RUSS. By peace and quiet I meant—

JEANNIE. Sensible?

RUSS. Yeah... in a way.

JEANNIE. I'm usually sensible... I am... aren't I? I'm not tonight. Reasonable or sensible. Either. Either...?

RUSS. You know what you need?

JEANNIE. No, I don't *(Firmly.)* I saw a lawyer, my cousin Ned Carlson... I'm getting a legal separation.

RUSS. We'll talk about it in the morning.

JEANNIE. He said he would make all the necessary arrange—

RUSS. Come to bed. *(She tenses. He begins to gently caress her.)* I love you... I need you. Who else would put up with me?

JEANNIE. You want me to answer that?

RUSS. Hey. C'mon.

(RUSS takes her head in his hands and kisses her and through the following continues to kiss and caress her.)

JEANNIE. You're not changing my mind about anything...

RUSS. *(Drawing her up into his arms.)* First there was Cleopatra...

JEANNIE. You have to apologize to my Dad for hitting him.

RUSS. Then came Scarlett O'Hara...

JEANNIE. You have to, Russ.

RUSS. Forever Amber.

JEANNIE. Honey, you do. Please promise.

RUSS. He hit me first, honey...

JEANNIE. He was defending...

RUSS. Blanche DuBois...

JEANNIE. His son, his family—

RUSS. ... and now...

JEANNIE. His patriotism—

RUSS. Out of the shadows comes Jeannie Brown Calhoun.

JEANNIE. He's an old man. You're younger... stronger...

RUSS. You bet...

JEANNIE. *(Returning his kiss.)* I'll stay the night if you promise to apologize... *(With familiar insinuation.)* "... out of the shadows... Jeannie Brown Cal—"

RUSS. *(Steps back from her.)* You'll let me make love to

you just as long as I apologize to dear old Dad.

JEANNIE. Yes.

RUSS. Go home.

JEANNIE. You said this was my home.

RUSS. A mistake.

JEANNIE. *(Angry.)* He was so right about you.

RUSS. "Brain damaged veteran?" *(Halfhearted menace.)* Ahhhhhhhh!

JEANNIE. Yes.

RUSS. Go. *(Grabs up beer.)* Go back to the old—

JEANNIE. I am. I'm going. It's cold out there, and it's dark... but I'm not afraid. You don't even care how I got here. I walked.

RUSS. You walked?

JEANNIE. I walked.

RUSS. I'll drive you.

(RUSS sets down beer, gets his jacket.)

JEANNIE. I don't want you to. I'm not afraid of the dark. The moon and the stars have always been my friends as long as I can remember, they care about me. Not like some people I know.

RUSS. C'mon.

(RUSS attempts to take JEANNIE by the arm.)

JEANNIE. I said NO!

(JEANNIE swings her shoulder bag, hitting RUSS in the face.)

RUSS. OW! Damn it! What've you got in there?

JEANNIE. A flashlight. *(Tentative.)* Did I hurt you?

RUSS. Your father punched me, your brother punched me, you slug me with a goddamn flashlight... *Damn.*

JEANNIE. *(Lacking conviction.)* You deserve it...

RUSS. Don't try it again—Get out of here! GO. WALK.

JEANNIE. I thought you were giving me a ride...

RUSS. *(Tossing off his jacket.)* You got here walking... go back walking.

JEANNIE. I'm not afraid.

RUSS. Why should you be? You got the moon, the stars and a forty pound flashlight.

JEANNIE. *(Opens the door.)* You've broken my heart. You know that?

RUSS. Geezuz...

JEANNIE. And do you know something? I hope that that Fat Freddy not only gets you fired but that he comes back and shoots you.

(JEANNIE exits.)

(BLACKOUT)

(Music.)

Scene 3

(Later that same night, about 2 A.M. The room is bathed in moonlight. There is a knock at the door. No response. Then

a second knock. The door opens. DIANE enters, closing the door after her.)

DIANE. *(Loud whisper.)* Russ? *(No response.)* RUSS!

RUSS. *(Offstage.)* Shit.

DIANE. Russ?

RUSS. What?

DIANE. It's me. Diane.

RUSS. No kidding.

DIANE. Are you alone?

RUSS. No. My wife's here. Will you go now?

DIANE. *(Turns on a light.)* She's not here. Is she? *(RUSS appears in the bedroom doorway. He is pulling on a robe.)* You're alone. You're a liar.

RUSS. It wouldn't stop you.

DIANE. I woke you.

RUSS. Yeah...

DIANE. Thanks for calling me.

RUSS. It's almost... 2 A.M. Why are you here?

DIANE. *You* called *me.*

RUSS. I called you because your father's walking around with half a million bucks and a gun, *I didn't invite you over at 2 in the—*

DIANE. *(Overlapping.)* What happened? Why is your face so swollen?

RUSS. I ran into a door...

DIANE. Another—

RUSS. Yeah, another door—*Why are you here*? Did he have an accident? —*What*?

DIANE. He's home in bed watching some stupid old movie. I went there after you called. He said he'd come to see you...

but there was no money or a gun.

RUSS. He's a liar.

DIANE. He said he talked to you, yes, but it was none of my business what you talked about. He was not happy that you'd called me... told me to get the hell out so he could watch Ida Lupino kill herself—What *did* you talk about?

RUSS. He offered me half a million bucks to get unmarried... and marry you... or I can have the Odeon and the Majestic or a partnership in the real estate business or the trucking company or the cab company or any other company he's got or will get.

DIANE. *(Pause.)* God...

RUSS. Generous, huh?

DIANE. *(Pause.)* I'm embarrassed.

RUSS. *You*? Why? You're your father's daughter.

DIANE. Oh, shut up. *(Riled.)* Ohhh, Id like to go back there right now and kick in his TV... and kick him, too. If he weren't going back into the hospital in the morning I would. I don't know where his mind is!

RUSS. On vacation?

DIANE. *(Shrugs. Pause.)* I do know that this time he's really scared. Know what the bigshot did? Bought the new altar for St. Joseph's— Can you believe it? Gets him one of those shiny, copper plaques... "donated by Federigo Caputo". *(Chuckles.)* And every Sunday he's going to mass again... a miracle... and every Monday, come rain or shine or snow, he drives to the cemetery and puts fresh flowers on my mother's grave... he couldn't stand her. Religion has come back with a vengeance. *(Pause.)* So what did you say to him? All those offers.

(DIANE sits.)

RUSS. I said no.

DIANE. He was trying to buy you for me.

RUSS. Wants his daughter happy.

DIANE. You can't go around buying people for—

RUSS. He loves you.

DIANE. And that makes it acceptable?

RUSS. Who said it was acceptable?

DIANE. He's going...

RUSS. Nuts.

DIANE. No. It's all those pain killers they give him... they make him—

RUSS. Nuts.

DIANE. He's not nuts, Russ, not really... he's just been... so blue. Who wouldn't be? This has given him some kind of... distraction...?

RUSS. Coming here tonight?

DIANE. *(Rises.)* I can't believe he did this.

(DIANE removes her coat.)

RUSS. Diane—

DIANE. Okay. So he's a little... tilted.

RUSS. Just hurry up and find the money and, more important, find the gun before he shoots me.

DIANE. How can he shoot you? He'll be in the hospital.

RUSS. When he gets out.

DIANE. *If* he gets—

RUSS. *(Overlapping.)* He's capable of using that gun. You told me he—

DIANE. *(Overlapping.)* When he was young, maybe.

RUSS. —murdered people.

DIANE. I never said *murdered.* He lived in the slums, he was caught up with a lot of riffraff, he had to defend himself, that's what I—

RUSS. You said—

DIANE. I said *maybe*, that's what I said, Russ.

RUSS. *(Overlapping.)* Find the money, find the gun. *(Picks up her coat.)* Try the trunk of his car... where he used to stuff the dead bodies.

DIANE. His car is new... '52 Chevy. Clean and shiny... not a bloodstain in the trunk. I do a monthly check.

RUSS. You find this funny?

DIANE. You used to say you didn't care whether you lived or died.

RUSS. That's because I was hanging around with you.

DIANE. *(Straightforward.)* Not so, no. With me, no more nightmares. You never slept better in your life. *(Pause.)* You said.

RUSS. *(Pause.)* I said. *(Silence. Near the front door he now holds up her coat, offering to help her into it. She backs away. Then he just tosses it to her. She catches it, and tosses it aside. Pause.)* You're all dressed up.

DIANE. *(Pause.)* Like it?

RUSS. You look terrific.

DIANE. Thank you.

RUSS. Something special?

DIANE. Sort of.

RUSS. Anybody I know?

DIANE. No.

RUSS. You sure?

DIANE. A man from Newport.

RUSS. Big shot?

DIANE. Of course.
RUSS. Getting up in the world.
DIANE. Always.
RUSS. Where'd you go?
DIANE. Out to dinner.
RUSS. Just dinner?
DIANE. A *late* dinner.
RUSS. Where?
DIANE. The Greenwich Inn.
RUSS. I thought that closed.
DIANE. Only for three weeks. They redecorated.
RUSS. How's it look redecorated?
DIANE. The same.
RUSS. The food still good?
DIANE. Uh huh.
RUSS. What did you have? Shrimp?
DIANE. *(Pause.)* Uh huh.
RUSS. *(Pause.)* What did your friend have?
DIANE. *(Pause.)* Shrimp.
RUSS. *(Pause.)* Friendly.
DIANE. Of course. *(Pause.)* A client. Real estate business. You don't have to be jealous.
RUSS. Who's jealous?
DIANE. I've been faithful to you, I told you.
RUSS. Not so. Thanksgiving weekend? A little lusty sacrifice for your country?
DIANE. What a memory.
RUSS. You tell secrets, they're not secrets anymore.

(They study one another. Impasse. Again he picks up her coat, holds it for her. Reluctantly, she slides into it.)

DIANE. You called me because you wanted to see me. My father gave you the excuse.

RUSS. *(Overlapping.)* Diane. I called you because your father was walking around with all that money and a gun.

DIANE. *(Simultaneously.)* —that money and a gun. It gave us both an excuse to see each other.

RUSS. Goodnight. I'm going back to bed.

DIANE. Am I invited? *(He halts.)* Look at it this way. Fat Freddy gets out of the hospital and shoots you dead. Then you'd regret we didn't have a last night together. *(Pause.)* No need for regrets. *(Pause.)* I can't keep throwing myself at you like this. Why are we playing games? We never played games. I hate playing games.

RUSS. Since when? *(Suddenly she sits, sighs. Pause.)* What?

DIANE. *(Pause.)* I feel like crying.

RUSS. Fat Freddy? *(She nods.)* So cry. *(Pause.)* I've never seen you cry.

DIANE. I can cry.

RUSS. Fat Freddy said.

DIANE. Did he. *(Pause.)* Well... he won't shoot you because he won't get out of the hospital this time.

RUSS. He won't die. He bought that new altar for St. Joseph's. That's, at least, a ten year guarantee.

DIANE. Ha, ha. This morning Dr. Russo told me... it doesn't look good.

RUSS. He always tells you that.

DIANE. How many times have I been through this in the last two years? Will he live, will he die, will he live, will he... you know... all those nights sitting with me at the hospital. *(Pause.)* You'd sit there... holding my hand. You were so nice.

RUSS. I'm a nice guy.

DIANE. *(Nods.)* You are. *(Pause. Sighs. Realization.)* Oh, Russ. I'm depressed.

RUSS. *(Pause.)* C'mon. *(Pause.)* C'mon, I'll cheer you up.

(RUSS gestures toward the bedroom.)

DIANE. Forget it. I don't want charity.

RUSS. A minute ago—

DIANE. A minute ago was a minute ago. Persuade me.

RUSS. Since when do you need persuas—

DIANE. Right now.

RUSS. *(Pause. Sings.)* "*Baby... baby, baby...*"

DIANE. That's fine.

(DIANE rises. They quickly come together. A long kiss. Then they break. She wriggles out of her coat, he crosses the room, turns out the light. Together they move toward the bedroom, discarding their clothes along the way.)

(BLACKOUT)

(Music.)

END OF ACT I

ACT II

Scene 1

(Three days later. Afternoon. About 1 P.M. The living room has now been stripped, including a large floor rug. What's left? The overstuffed armchair, a floor lamp, end table with telephone, an ottoman, bookcase, the handmade dining room table, and the three attached theatre chairs.)

(As lights rise: JEANNIE comes out of the bedroom carrying a small bedlamp and a large paper bag which she sets down by the front door. She looks around her, then goes into the kitchen, almost immediately returning with a toaster which she puts into the paper bag. She puts on her jacket, picks up the lamp, the paper bag and her shoulder bag. The front door opens, FAT FREDDY enters. JEANNIE gasps.)

FAT FREDDY. Easy.
JEANNIE. You scared me.

(JEANNIE immediately notes the briefcase FAT FREDDY is carrying.)

FAT FREDDY. Sorry. I'm Fat Freddy.
JEANNIE. I know.
FAT FREDDY. I've met you at the Olde Rock Bank. You

was helpin' President Henderson for me.

JEANNIE. Uh huh...

FAT FREDDY. When I met you you was Jeannie Brown, now you're Jeannie Calhoun.

JEANNIE. Brown in my maiden name. I'm getting it back.

FAT FREDDY. Those two guys in the van said to tell ya they're leavin'.

JEANNIE. Oh.

(JEANNIE moves past FAT FREDDY to the door as if to go out.)

FAT FREDDY. They're gone. What happened here?

JEANNIE. Do you always just walk into people's houses?

FAT FREDDY. If the door's unlocked, sure. *(Referring to the stripped room.)* You been busy.

JEANNIE. My father said it was the only thing I could do... under the circumstances. I'm putting it in storage until I... I did what was right. I only took what belonged to me... yes, wedding presents, yes... some things you can't chop in half. My hus... Russ... you know him, he's my husband but he isn't... as far as I'm concerned. We're separated. But I don't want his name anymore because of... things... some of which you're familiar with... and connected to. I didn't take anything that was originally here, originally his. I'm not that kind of person.

FAT FREDDY. Then Russ isn't here.

JEANNIE. Would I be doing this... if he was?

FAT FREDDY. Do you know where he is?

JEANNIE. At the Majestic. On Tuesdays he works from noon to midnight, the twelve hour shift. Well, almost twelve—

(Still holding onto the front doorknob.) He's not here. Aren't you leaving?

FAT FREDDY. I'll wait.

JEANNIE. He won't be home until late.

FAT FREDDY. You said.

(FAT FREDDY sets down briefcase, sits in the overstuffed chair.)

JEANNIE. I was going.

FAT FREDDY. Go.

JEANNIE. I don't want to leave you alone in—

FAT FREDDY. I won't steal anything. You took most of it anyway.

JEANNIE. *(Curious.)* Aren't you supposed to be in the hospital?

FAT FREDDY. Been... and back. I've got a cold. They can't do anything when you got a cold, they think you might get pneumonia. They release you, send you home. Let go of the doorknob, I promise not to harm you.

JEANNIE. You have a gun.

FAT FREDDY. I do?

JEANNIE. And you have that briefcase with you again.

FAT FREDDY. *(Pause.)* Huh?

JEANNIE. The other night... when you were talking to Russ... I was in there, in the bedroom. Neither of you knew, but I was... in there. I heard everything... well, not the beginning, I was asleep... but after that I heard... *everything*.

FAT FREDDY. Why didn't ya come out of hidin'?

JEANNIE. I was shocked. *(Boldly.)* Did you come to offer him money again, or did you come to shoot him?

FAT FREDDY. Any suggestions?

JEANNIE. Shoot him.

FAT FREDDY. *(Laughs.)* You're a vengeful girl.

JEANNIE. I didn't know I was.

FAT FREDDY. You don't look like a vengeful girl.

JEANNIE. I look like goody-two-shoes... that's what I look like. I smile a lot, I've always smiled... I thought it was important.

FAT FREDDY. Makes you likeable.

JEANNIE. I don't want to be likeable, I want to be loved. *(Restraining tears.)* Shoot him...

FAT FREDDY. You must really hate him.

JEANNIE. He broke my heart.

FAT FREDDY. Good reason. My cousin Louie caught his wife with the gas man. Louie shot her. She never broke his heart again.

JEANNIE. *(Pause.)* Don't shoot Russ. I take it back.

FAT FREDDY. Well...

JEANNIE. Shooting a person is wrong... it's a crime... you can go to jail.

FAT FREDDY. They haven't caught me yet.

(FAT FREDDY sneezes.)

JEANNIE. God bless you.

FAT FREDDY. Thank you.

JEANNIE. I can call the police... I can say you have a deadly weapon... *(He sneezes again.)* ... God bless you... with intent to kill.

FAT FREDDY. C'mon, Jeannie, I'm not gonna shoot him. That was the old days. This is 1952... guns are mainly used now to scare people. *(Blows his nose.)* Anyway, I don't have a gun.

JEANNIE. Last time you were here I heard you say that and you *did*... have a gun.

FAT FREDDY. Oh. Well... *(Pause.)* Okay. You've been honest with me, Jeannie, so I'll be honest with you. You're right, I do. But you never use it, you just threaten with it. Understand? Sit down, Jeannie.

JEANNIE. Why?

FAT FREDDY. Put down all that. Take off you jacket.

JEANNIE. *(Sets down the bag and the lamp.)* I... I should go.

FAT FREDDY. Please. Sit, Jeannie. We'll talk a little.

JEANNIE. *(Pause.)* Just for a minute or so.

FAT FREDDY. Good, good. *(JEANNIE looks around for a place to sit. Her choices are few. She sits in one of the theatre chairs.)* There. There you go. We'll get acquainted.

JEANNIE. It's as if... you're the host... and I'm the visitor...

FAT FREDDY. It's like that wherever I go, Jeannie. I make myself at home.

JEANNIE. Then you are here again to make him another money offer?

FAT FREDDY. You know, you're not only a likeable girl, you're pretty, too. You are. Very pretty.

JEANNIE. Thank you.

FAT FREDDY. You're welcome. You got a special smile. Look at that. *(Laughs.)* Yeah... yeah, you do.

JEANNIE. Thank you.

FAT FREDDY. You're welcome. Now. Tell me about yourself.

JEANNIE. Pardon?

FAT FREDDY. Tell me about yourself.

JEANNIE. You didn't answer my question.

FAT FREDDY. What question was that?

JEANNIE. Offering the money again to—

FAT FREDDY. Oh. Oh... oh. On the fence, on the fence. You know what's funny, Jeannie? You're easy to talk to. You fine me easy to talk to?

JEANNIE. Yes... yes, I do. Isn't that funny?

FAT FREDDY. Yeah, it is, isn't it?

JEANNIE. Yes... because we're enemies.

FAT FREDDY. You and me? Naw. No... no. Maybe on opposite sides, but enemies... not in a thousand years. Now. I'd like to hear.

JEANNIE. Pardon?

FAT FREDDY. About yourself. Tell me.

JEANNIE. Oh. What would you like to know?

FAT FREDDY. Your hopes, your dreams...

JEANNIE. Oh. *(Pause.)* From the beginning?

FAT FREDDY. Well, you don't—

JEANNIE. I was born on a rainy day, March 3rd, Pisces... very rainy, my father told me. My full name is Jeannie Marilyn Brown. I was named after my paternal grandmother Jeannie Brown and my maternal grandmother Marilyn Marley. My mother wanted to name me Samantha... but my father said it was too high toned. I first walked at the age of—

FAT FREDDY. 'Scuse me, Jeannie. Let's kinda jump along... get a little more up-to-date.

JEANNIE. *(Overlapping.)* Oh. Oh, all right... fine. Let's see. You mean like highlights?

FAT FREDDY. Highlights? Well, maybe—

JEANNIE. All right. Let's see. Uh huh. In the fourth grade I lost the spelling bee to Hazel Dean... but the next year, luckily, I beat her, I was so happy! Oh, and in the sixth grade I got one of the leads in the Christmas pageant. I played Lolli the elf, and I sang a solo. *(Sings.) "I'm Lolli the elf, I'm here to bring joy—"*

FAT FREDDY. I'm sure you was a triumph as Lolli the elf, Jeannie, but that ain't exactly up-to-date. Like the present.

JEANNIE. Oh.

FAT FREDDY. Now. Today. Like earlier you said you're gettin' ya own name back?

JEANNIE. Oh. Yes. Definitely.

FAT FREDDY. How are ya gettin' ya own name back?

JEANNIE. I'm getting a divorce. Didn't I say that?— I guess not.

FAT FREDDY. *(Overlapping.)* You're not Catholic?

JEANNIE. No. Episcopalian.

FAT FREDDY. How are ya goin' about gettin' your divorce?

JEANNIE. Well, I've talked to my cousin Ned Carlson. He's a lawyer. He'll be helping me.

FAT FREDDY. Maybe I could help you.

JEANNIE. You? You're against me.

FAT FREDDY. I'm not *against* you, Jeannie, I'm just *for* my daughter. You can bet your life if she wasn't I'd be against *her* and for *you* but she is so I am.

JEANNIE. *(Pause.)* I don't follow you.

FAT FREDDY. Just listen, Jeannie, you listen. Now. People go through life... they get on one track... they never discover they can get on another track.

JEANNIE. *(Pause.)* I don't follow you.

FAT FREDDY. Hopes and dreams, Jeannie, like you said, hopes and dreams. Now, Jeannie... you know money. 'Course, you know money. You handle it every day at the Olde Rock Bank. Right?

JEANNIE. Yes...

FAT FREDDY. You follow that?

JEANNIE. I follow that... but...

FAT FREDDY. Good. Now. You handle it every day... but *you* don't have *it* to do with as *you* want. You follow that?

JEANNIE. I follow that...

FAT FREDDY. Good. Everybody wants to make money, Jeannie, 'cause money gets them things, money gives them freedom, money gives them power. But everybody, *most* people get sidetracked. *Because...* they *stay-on-one-track.*

JEANNIE. *(Pause.)* I... I don't—

FAT FREDDY. You will, you will, just listen. Now. Some smart ones—like myself—finally figured out you can be on one track... and suddenly *become aware* you can *switch directions fast...* go any which way.

JEANNIE. I've never liked trains.

FAT FREDDY. Forget the tracks, forget the trains, I'm gettin' to the point. The point I'm gettin' to is this, Jeannie: You can make *rearrangements*. That's my point.

JEANNIE. Trains always make me nauseous. I'm not sure why.

FAT FREDDY. *(Overlapping.)* Forget the trains, Jeannie, I'm talkin' about—

JEANNIE. I'm not afraid to fly. I love planes...

FAT FREDDY. Forget the trains, forget the planes, I'm—

JEANNIE. I've never been in a plane.

FAT FREDDY. You will, you will. *Jeannie.* I'm talkin' about rearrangements now... *for you.* Listen. Just follow me. *(Pause.)* Now. You can speed up the process. Your divorce. And make some money. *(Pause.)* Freedom. *(Pause.)* Power. *(Pause.)* You follow me now? You do! *(Enthused, laughing.)* I can see it in your face. Look at you... ready to leap! *(Laughs. Pause. Serious again.)* You can make the leap. Listen. *(Pause.)* Now. I want my daughter's happiness. She wants... Russ, she's gonna get him—Wait! Which is okay by you because he broke your heart and you hate him. Jeannie, it's to your advantage, sweetness, if you're on my side... Wait! Listen! You said you had a broken heart. We meet, I'm here, God's *will*!... I can mend it. It's simple, Jeannie. You're young, you're pretty, you're sweet, you're *so sweet...* you're deservin'! You just told me you was born on a rainy day. Do the rest of the days of your life have to be rainy? NO!... not even when it's rainin'.

JEANNIE. *(Pause.)* I'm not sure I follow—

FAT FREDDY. *(Overlapping.)* Jeannie... rearrangements. For you... f*rom me*... you'll thank me later. Now. I'll give you the half million bucks... free... and I'll get you to Reno to get your divorce. You'll take up residency there for only six weeks, then you'll be free of the man who doesn't deserve you... You follow me, you know what I'm talkin' about, you do, sweetness, you're no dummy.

JEANNIE. *(Pause.)* I can't go to Reno...

FAT FREDDY. 'Course you can.

JEANNIE. ... my job.

FAT FREDDY. You'll have a half a million beautiful bucks... you can quit.

JEANNIE. Quit my job?

FAT FREDDY. *(Overlapping.)* You can quit, have a new life, do whatever you want with that kind of dough. First class all the way.

JEANNIE. No, Mr. Caputo.

(JEANNIE rises.)

FAT FREDDY. Fat Freddy, sweetness.

JEANNIE. Your... rearrangements... whatever you call them... no.

FAT FREDDY. Jeannie, you're an intelligent girl—

JEANNIE. I'd never consider it...

FAT FREDDY. Use your head. Do you know what you can do with—

JEANNIE. *Unless*... you apologize to me.

FAT FREDDY. *(Pause.)* Apologize? For what?

JEANNIE. For insulting me. That night... you were talking to Russ... you insulted me. Personally. You said I was... flat chested.

FAT FREDDY. No. I said you had no tits.

JEANNIE. I want an apology... and they're breasts, not what you call them.

FAT FREDDY. *(Overlapping.)* Listen, if I'm offering you half a million bucks, I can call a tit a tit, understand?

JEANNIE. I demand an apology.

FAT FREDDY. Why? What I said is true... isn't it?

JEANNIE. I am *not* flat chested.

FAT FREDDY. Seein's believin'.

JEANNIE. *(Non-plussed.)* You want me to... *show you*?

FAT FREDDY. You're the one tryin' to prove to me... but you're not that brave, are you.

JEANNIE. I'm brave. Look what I did here. I took what belonged to me.

FAT FREDDY. Pushed to it by your father.

JEANNIE. But I did it. But what you speak of is... unspeakable. It isn't bravery... it's just... improper.

FAT FREDDY. Are you a prude?

JEANNIE. No.

FAT FREDDY. Then show me. *(Pause.)* Make your point... points? *(Pause.)* I didn't bring this up, you did.

(JEANNIE hesitates, then removes her jacket. Then she begins to undue her blouse, stops herself, looks about her as if someone might be watching. She notices the curtainless windows, steps aside from them. She's having second thoughts, then plunges on. She shows him, of course still wearing her brassiere, but nevertheless exposed. Silence.)

FAT FREDDY. Come closer.

JEANNIE. No. Please apologize.

FAT FREDDY. *(Pause.)* Lovely... lovely, Jeannie.

JEANNIE. Please apologize.

FAT FREDDY. You're right, oh, I apologize, sweetness. *(Pause.)* If I were younger... I'd take you...

JEANNIE. Mr.—

FAT FREDDY. ... dancing.

JEANNIE. *(Quickly moving away, buttoning up. Shocked at herself.) I've never done anything... like this.*

FAT FREDDY. I have that effect on people. I bring out their... adventure.

JEANNIE. I must be going crazy, too.

FAT FREDDY. You're not crazy, you're brave... standin'

up for your own rights. You got me to apologize... Lovely, Jeannie... and that makes you ready to accept my proposition.

JEANNIE. What proposition?

FAT FREDDY. The money, the divorce, rearrangements. But, Jeannie, there's a slight hitch. We do it right away, you go *today*... fly to Reno... the money's yours.

(FAT FREDDY rises, and soon puts briefcase on the table.)

JEANNIE. How can I—

FAT FREDDY. You get on a plane, you just do it, sweetness.

JEANNIE. How can I—

FAT FREDDY. You can. Look what you just did? If you can bravely show your... your cleavage, then you can sure as hell get on a plane.

JEANNIE. My job.

FAT FREDDY. You take a leave of absence from—

JEANNIE. I took today off, I called in sick. I lied... so I could do this. I said I had the flu. Please don't tell anyone at the bank, I know you're friendly with President Henderson...

FAT FREDDY. My lips are sealed. I'll arrange everything in no time flat. Where's that smile? Just trust me.

JEANNIE. I can't. Just get up and go so fast?—I'm sensible, I'm reasonable, I can't. How can I do it?

FAT FREDDY. Come here. Open the briefcase. *(She hesitates, then opens it.)* Now can you do it?

JEANNIE. *(Looking at the money.)* I can do it.

FAT FREDDY. Good girl. *(Goes to the telephone.)* What's the number of the bank?

JEANNIE. 675-1112. But—

FAT FREDDY. Shhhh.

(FAT FREDDY dials.)

JEANNIE. *(Pause.)* Mr. Fat Freddy—

FAT FREDDY. Shhhh. President Henderson...

JEANNIE. Oh...

FAT FREDDY. Fat Freddy.

JEANNIE. Don't...

FAT FREDDY. Don't worry, I'll take care of—

JEANNIE. But—

FAT FREDDY. —Hello, Tom, how are ya?... I've got a cold... Tom, I need a favor, Tom. One of your tellers, Jeannie Brown Calhoun wants... I know she's not in today, she needs a leave of absence... Tom, it's personal.

JEANNIE. *(Grabbing the receiver from him.)* I quit. This is Jeannie Brown Calhoun, you never liked me anyway. I quit!

(JEANNIE hands receiver back to FAT FREDDY.)

FAT FREDDY. Talk to you soon, Tom.

(FAT FREDDY hangs up.)

JEANNIE. I quit...

FAT FREDDY. *(Dialing again.)* I think so.

JEANNIE. I can't believe I did that.

FAT FREDDY. You did it, sweetness.

JEANNIE. I said I quit and I quit!

FAT FREDDY. Ambrose, it's me again.

(FAT FREDDY sneezes.)

JEANNIE. God bless you.

FAT FREDDY. What we talked about is happening...

JEANNIE. I was brave.

FAT FREDDY. Mexico! Don'tcha need a passport? —Forget Mexico.

JEANNIE. *(Thrilled with herself.)* I *am* brave!

FAT FREDDY. *(Impatient.)* Yeah, the flight from La Guardia to Chicago to Reno, yeah... Yeah, I'll hold on.

JEANNIE. I hated that bank.

FAT FREDDY. *(To JEANNIE.)* 'Course, you did. Who wants to count other people's money.

JEANNIE. I feel...

FAT FREDDY. Free.

JEANNIE. Yes! Oh, Mr. Fat Freddy... *(He sneezes again.)* ... God bless you... You give me courage.

FAT FREDDY. I'm also givin' ya half a million bucks.

JEANNIE. I did hate that job.

FAT FREDDY. *(Overlapping.)* Yeah, Ambrose...

JEANNIE. "Next, please."

FAT FREDDY. Yeah.

JEANNIE. "How would you like that, sir? Tens? Twenties?"

FAT FREDDY. Jeannie Calhoun... yeah, a she, yeah...

JEANNIE. *(Puts the open briefcase on the table, and is soon gripping it.)* "I'm sorry. You have insufficient funds to cover that check."

FAT FREDDY. Oh, yeah?

JEANNIE. "I'm sorry, I don't have the authorization to do that."

FAT FREDDY. *(Overlapping.)* What the hell's that mean?

JEANNIE. "I'm sorry, you'll have to speak to one of the officers."

FAT FREDDY. *You* fly her to La Guardia if you have to.

JEANNIE. *(Growing more elated.)* "No, I'm sorry, I won't help you!"

FAT FREDDY. Who do you think you're talkin' to?

JEANNIE. "This window is closed...!"

FAT FREDDY. Don't give me that *crap.*

JEANNIE. *(Reaching a peak.)* "FOREVER!"

FAT FREDDY. Just do it or I'll burn your fuckin' house down.

(BLACKOUT)

(Music.)

Scene 2

(That same night. About midnight. RUSS, with his jacket on, is reading a note. DIANE enters from outside.)

DIANE. Hi, baby. *(Pauses.)* What happened here?

(RUSS hands her the note, exits into the kitchen, turns on the light. DIANE reads the note. She is not displeased.)

RUSS. *(Returning.)* The stove and the refrigerator are about all that's left in there.

DIANE. Surprise... !

RUSS. *(Pause.)* I can't believe she did this...

DIANE. She did it.

RUSS. I can't believe it.

DIANE. This room looks better. Less cluttered... like it used to look.

RUSS. She says she took what belongs to her...

DIANE. You'd know... I wouldn't.

RUSS. She's flying to Reno.

DIANE. I read it.

RUSS. To get a divorce.

DIANE. Says right here.

(DIANE sets note down on the table.)

RUSS. *(Pause. Picking up the note.)* She wrote this at two this afternoon. *(Pause.)* How do you get to Reno?

DIANE. Airplane.

RUSS. From Boston? New York?

DIANE. Either... ?

RUSS. I'm going after her.

DIANE. After she robbed you?

RUSS. I can stop her.

DIANE. It's almost midnight. She's got a big head start.

RUSS. You think this is the way to get things settled?

DIANE. How's the bedroom? I hope she left the bed.

RUSS. Her father. *(Moving toward the telephone.)* He's behind all this.

DIANE. *(At the bedroom doorway.)* Ahhh. It's still here. Goody.

RUSS. *(Overlapping/Dialing.)* The old jackass would do anything to get her away from me.

DIANE. *(Overlapping.)* Speaking of old jackasses... guess who's sleeping in your bed? *My* mystery solved.

RUSS. Fat Freddy... ?

DIANE. In person. I never thought of looking here. *(RUSS replaces the receiver, starts toward the bedroom, stops, turns back to the telephone, then turns to her. Pause.)* What?

RUSS. Him. Here. Not *her* father, *your* father.

DIANE. You're right. That's him.

RUSS. You know what I meant. Did you arrange all this with him?

DIANE. Did I—All what? This?

RUSS. This, yeah. And getting my wife to go to Reno. That cost—

DIANE. *(Riled.)* Why don't you ask the big shot? (shouting into the bedroom.) HEY, BIG SHOT, WAKE UP! We've got a man here with a problem!

RUSS. That's far-fetched?

DIANE. *What*?

RUSS. *(Aroused.)* You and your father. Manipulating me? Manipulating Jeannie?

FAT FREDDY. *(From offstage.)* Where am I?

DIANE. In heaven.

FAT FREDDY. Heaven? Can't be. I hear my daughter's voice.

(As FAT FREDDY appears in the bedroom doorway, RUSS begins to move restlessly about the room.)

DIANE. How are you?

FAT FREDDY. Rotten. You woke me up.

DIANE. Where did you disappear to this morning?

FAT FREDDY. I've got a miserable cold.

DIANE. Nobody knew where you'd—

FAT FREDDY. They released me from the hospital, I had things to do... and then I came here to talk to Russ and he wasn't here.

RUSS. Jeannie was.

FAT FREDDY. Yeah, cleanin' out the joint. What time is it?

DIANE. Midnight.

FAT FREDDY. My watch stopped. Is that a sign? It is... *definite* sign. Time's runnin' out on me.

DIANE. *(Overlapping.)* I've been looking for you all day, all night... I was frantic.

FAT FREDDY. *(Overlapping.)* Midnight. I slept a long time.

(FAT FREDDY sniffles.)

DIANE. Did you hear what I said?

FAT FREDDY. I heard you. Get me a glass of water.

DIANE. Please.

FAT FREDDY. Just *get me a glass of water.*

(DIANE is about to respond, checks herself, and exits into the kitchen.)

RUSS. What about my wife?

FAT FREDDY. I'm glad she didn't take the bed. Good mattress. Best sleep I've had in months.

RUSS. Look, Mr. Caputo—

FAT FREDDY. She wrote you a note, sonny, you got it. She was here when I got here... gettin' the van filled, I had nothin' to do with *that. But—*

RUSS. But you have a lot to do with Reno.

FAT FREDDY. I have everything to do with Reno. She must be almost there by now. *(Takes out pills.)* HURRY UP WITH THAT WATER, I'M DRY AS A BONE. *(Sits in his favorite chair.)* She was already dealin' with a divorce lawyer... her cousin Ned somebody.

RUSS. *(Overlapping.)* You just got things moving faster.

FAT FREDDY. Right. What d'ya do? Get into another fight?

RUSS. *(As DIANE returns.)* Not yet.

(FAT FREDDY sneezes.)

DIANE. God bless you.

FAT FREDDY. Thanks, angel face. He's agitated.

(FAT FREDDY takes the glass of water, takes pills.)

DIANE. *(In reference to the pills.)* You took three. You're only supposed to take two at—

FAT FREDDY. Extra one for good behavior.

DIANE. *(To RUSS.)* He eats those pills the way he used to eat candy. *(FAT FREDDY sneezes again.)* God bless you.

FAT FREDDY. Cold's getting worse.

RUSS. You gave her the money to go to Reno. You arranged it all.

FAT FREDDY. Every detail. From Hillsgrove to La Guardia to Chicago to Reno. You wouldn't accept my proposition so I tried her. Bingo! Rearrangements! Five hundred thousand bucks in cash. 'Course, she had to move like lightnin' or no deal. She moved like lightnin'.

DIANE. *(Overlapping.) Five hundred thousand...*

FAT FREDDY. *(Overlapping. To RUSS.)* You should've taken the money while you had the chance, sonny.

DIANE. *(Overlapping.) You gave her—*

FAT FREDDY. It's gonna be clear for you two to be together again... live happily ever after. It's done. Grab it.

DIANE. *(To RUSS.)* You were right. *(To FAT FREDDY.)* You are nuts.

FAT FREDDY. Don't talk stupid.

RUSS. You think I'm gonna go along with all this... all this...

FAT FREDDY. Go along with *what's done*? You have to. Your wife doesn't love you. Gets offered a nice chunk of money and what does she do? Quits her job, gets on a plane... Zoom! That's love?

RUSS. *(Overlapping.)* She took the money from you because she's—

FAT FREDDY. A broken heart, I know, she confided in me. But broken hearts mend fast when you get big bucks. Fact is she took it, *went*, I didn't hold a gun to her head. So. You made a mistake, I—

RUSS. *I* made—

FAT FREDDY. *(Overlapping.) I* cleared it up for you. You and Diane can retrace your steps, get back together... where you belong.

RUSS. I belong where *I say* I—

FAT FREDDY. Pride's a pain in the ass.

DIANE. God.

FAT FREDDY. *(Overlapping.)* Don't let pride rob you of

the happiness you're entitled to.

DIANE. *(Overlapping.)* You didn't have to butt in. Everything was working out.

RUSS. What do you mean, "Everything was working out?"

DIANE. *(Overlapping.)* Between you and me. *(To FAT FREDDY.)* We were getting there on our own time.

FAT FREDDY. What time? Where's your memory? In the truckin' office I caught you cryin' like a baby, cryin' over him... What to do?—What to do?—

RUSS. You *did* plan this with him.

DIANE. Are you nuts? He's nuts, I'm not nuts!

FAT FREDDY. Listen, *ingrate*!... I wanted to do something special for you before I croaked so don't tell me I'm *nuts*!

DIANE. Nuts.

FAT FREDDY. *I did it for you*! You wanted him, you got him.

RUSS. *Nobody's got me*!

FAT FREDDY. Who ya kiddin'? Once she makes up her mind, there's—

DIANE. Will you—

RUSS. *(Overlapping.) Nobody's got me*!

FAT FREDDY. What do they see in you? You ain't got a pot to piss in, you got about as much ambition as a duck's ass, you must have some pecker.

(RUSS lunges for FAT FREDDY, yanking him to his feet.)

DIANE. Russ! LET HIM GO! RUSS! *(RUSS lets him go. Angered.)* What were you going to do? Punch him out?

RUSS. *(Shaken.)* Why not.

DIANE. He's sick.

RUSS. He's not sick, he's dying.

DIANE. Shut up! Just keep your hands off him.

FAT FREDDY. *(Overlapping.)* Good you let go, sonny...

DIANE. Don't touch him again.

FAT FREDDY. *(Overlapping.)* Or I'd blow your guts out.

RUSS. You both better get out of here.

DIANE. *(Pause.)* What's that supposed to mean?

RUSS. Get out of here!

DIANE. *(Pause.)* I had nothing to do with—

RUSS. Sure you did. "Once she makes up her mind..."

FAT FREDDY. She's like me.

DIANE. No, I'm not like you.

RUSS. *(Overlapping.)* HEY! *(Pause.)* Get your father out of my house. *(Pause.)* Better idea...

(RUSS exits.)

DIANE. Russ... *(Opens front door.)* Russ, *where are you— (Pause.)* RUSS! *(Sound of car is heard pulling away from the house. Pause.)* He's going after her.

(DIANE closes door.)

FAT FREDDY. Naw.

DIANE. *Damn you.*

FAT FREDDY. It'll all work out.

DIANE. I hate you.

FAT FREDDY. No you don't.

DIANE. You just can't stay out of my business.

FAT FREDDY. Soon I'll be completely out of your business, and—

DIANE. Good! Because if you don't conk out this time I'll have you locked up for the rest—

FAT FREDDY. I'm not nuts!—You cut that—

DIANE. Half a million dollars?!

FAT FREDDY. A grand farewell *gift* for my—

DIANE. Stop it! Farewell. You've been *farewelling* for the last two years, putting me through the meat grinder every—

FAT FREDDY. I'm the one goin' through the meat grinder, not—

DIANE. Why didn't you just have her killed?

FAT FREDDY. You're not serious.

DIANE. Would've been cheaper.

FAT FREDDY. Hard to get away with that anymore... at least in this town.

DIANE. You don't see the insanity.

FAT FREDDY. *You cut-that-out*!

DIANE. And where did that money come from?

FAT FREDDY. Just say: "Thank you, Poppa"... is that so difficult?

DIANE. Thank you for what?! He's not here. Is he here? No! He's gone, she's gone, I'm thrilled!

FAT FREDDY. He's just—

DIANE. Answer me. Where did that money come—

FAT FREDDY. None of you business.

(FAT FREDDY sniffles.)

DIANE. It is my business because I run your business... *all* of them. The bank accounts *and* all the books better balance or—

FAT FREDDY. Be quiet. *(Sniffles.)* I've had that money for fifteen years.

DIANE. Did you rob a bank? *(FAT FREDDY sniffles again.)* Forget I asked. *(And sniffles again.)* Oh, blow your nose.

FAT FREDDY. You givin' *me* orders?

DIANE. You've got a cold, you're sniffling, blow your nose.

FAT FREDDY. *(Overlapping.)* Don't treat me like a child.

DIANE. *Don't* blow you nose.

(DIANE goes to the phone. FAT FREDDY blows his nose.)

FAT FREDDY. I think they injected me with something to give me a cold 'cause they knew they couldn't operate again. *(Coughs now.)* Yeah, Diane... right. Call Father De Maio... the Last Rites... won't be long now. *(Coughs again.)* Inside feels like I'm on two parallel train tracks...

DIANE. It's me... I found him.

FAT FREDDY. Climbin' up a mountain...

DIANE. Visiting friends.

FAT FREDDY. One track, my immortal soul...

DIANE. We're on our way now, Celia.

FAT FREDDY. The other track, my body... and when they hit the top of the mountain, that'll be—

DIANE. He's having visions.

FAT FREDDY. I'M NOT HAVING VISIONS!

DIANE. The Little Engine That Could.

FAT FREDDY. My body and soul, damn it!

DIANE. Hold on. *(To FAT FREDDY.)* Are you hungry?

FAT FREDDY. Who wants to know?

DIANE. The Pope.

FAT FREDDY. I'll tell her when I see her!

DIANE. Did you hear him?... Bye.

FAT FREDDY. *(Overlapping.)* Wait! Tell her scrambled eggs, toast, orange marmalade, bacon—

DIANE. Too late. She hung up.

FAT FREDDY. Damnit! Break the rules—Bacon!—

DIANE. Celia has been told—

FAT FREDDY. You come in with me, make sure I get some bacon no matter what the—

DIANE. (Exiting into the bedroom.) Fine. Let's go.

FAT FREDDY. Why'd you call her anyway?

DIANE. *(From offstage.)* Because she was worried.

FAT FREDDY. Worried. The old crow.

DIANE. The old crow is the best housekeeper you've ever had. Be grateful. Let's—

FAT FREDDY. Yeah, you're right there. Nobody's more devoted than Celia. I'm her life.

DIANE. *(Returning with his suit jacket, overcoat and hat.)* C'mon.

FAT FREDDY. When I'm gone she'll fall apart.

DIANE. Don't count on it.

FAT FREDDY. Like you'll fall apart.

(And through the rest of this scene DIANE attempts to remain low-keyed. Also during the following she makes a number of attempts to get him into his suit jacket, overcoat and hat.)

DIANE. Are you going to get out of that chair?

FAT FREDDY. Will you mourn me after I depart for places unknown?

DIANE. You know where you're going.

(DIANE indicates down.)

FAT FREDDY. *(Exploding.)* YOU SHOW ME THE PROPER RESPECT, HEAR ME?... *(He is up, but he sits right back down. Coughs a little.)* Or else... I'll leave everything to my brother and —

DIANE. Ha.

FAT FREDDY. That'll sizzle you.

DIANE. You wouldn't leave him a dead chicken. C'mon, let's go.

FAT FREDDY. You won't shed a tear, will you.

DIANE. AT your funeral? No. I'll dance. That's what you said...

FAT FREDDY. Oh... right.

DIANE. *(Overlapping.)* ... you wanted.

FAT FREDDY. Right. A band.

DIANE. You'll get it.

FAT FREDDY. A band at a funeral isn't unholy is it?

DIANE. I'll look it up.

(DIANE sits.)

FAT FREDDY. Where? The yellow pages?... Look it up... *(Pause.)* Father De Maio would know.

DIANE. I'll ask him.

FAT FREDDY. I thought you was callin' him before... to set up the Last Rites. How many times have I—

DIANE. Three.

FAT FREDDY. *(Suddenly shaken.)* I don't want to die. *(Pause.)* How come you don't say: "Stop talking that crap" anymore?

DIANE. Because-you-live!... and now you're hungry and Celia is waiting to cook you something.

FAT FREDDY. Celia's the best housekeeper, the best cook out of all of 'em... and the best in bed... the old crow. *(During the following list DIANE will mime with him the last four names.)* Better than Mona... Celeste... Irma... Milly... Madeline... Beatrice... and better than your mother. Your mother could cook...

DIANE. *(Pause.)* Uh huh.

FAT FREDDY. That was it. *(Pause.)* You know wherever I wind up... whatever part of heaven... *don't* roll your eyes... *heaven, whatever part...* I hope I'm nowhere near your mother. What a bore. Boy, was she borin'. Wasn't she?

DIANE. *(Pause.)* Yes.

(FAT FREDDY laughs, and in spite of herself DIANE begins to laugh with him.)

FAT FREDDY. She sure was. Not like us. Not like you and me, father and daughter. We're not boring... oh, no... we're special... you bet your boots. Remember how I'd get you to sing with me? She didn't like that. *(Sings.)* *"C'mon an' hear—"*

DIANE. No.

FAT FREDDY. Hey.

DIANE. No.

FAT FREDDY. I just spent half a million bucks on you. Can't you just give me the "boom-boom?" Will that kill you? *(Pause.)* Will it? Final request from—

DIANE. Go ahead.

FAT FREDDY.	DIANE.
"C'mon an' hear	
	Boom-Boom
C'mon an' hear	
	Boom-Boom

FAT FREDDY. (cont.)
Alexander's ragtime band

DIANE. (cont.)
Boom-da-Boom

FAT FREDDY.
C'mon an' hear

DIANE.
Boom-Boom

FAT FREDDY.
C'mon an' hear

DIANE.
Boom-Boom

FAT FREDDY.
It's the best band in the land

DIANE.
Boom-da-Boom

FAT FREDDY.
They can play the bugle call
Like you never heard before

DIANE.
Boom

FAT FREDDY.
So natural that you wanna go..."

(FAT FREDDY begins to cough, ending the song. DIANE rises. As the coughing spasm decreases:)

FAT FREDDY. *(cont.)* We were pretty good, huh?

(DIANE nods and gets him to drink some water.)

DIANE. *(Pause.)* C'mon... let's go. I'll get you home.

(DIANE readies his suit jacket.)

FAT FREDDY. You don't really hate me, do you, angel face?

(FAT FREDDY rises.)

DIANE. Yup.

FAT FREDDY. *(Snatches the suit jacket from her.)* I did it

for you, dummy! *(A spasm of pain leaves him breathless, but his anger overrides it.) Half a million bucks!*

(FAT FREDDY moves away from DIANE, gets into his suit jacket.)

DIANE. Give me the gun.
FAT FREDDY. What gun?

(FAT FREDDY gets into his overcoat.)

DIANE. The one you—Just give it to me.
FAT FREDDY. Why?
DIANE. For safe keeping.
FAT FREDDY. You wanna shoot me?
DIANE. It's a thought. Give it—
FAT FREDDY. *(Draws it out of his overcoat pocket.)* There's no bullets. Move. I just carry it around for effect. Move. *(She moves to the door, waits. Pause.)* I've always loved you, you know. You love me, too. *(Gets no response.)* Is it so painful to say you love your father?
DIANE. I want to get out of here.
FAT FREDDY. Say it.
DIANE. What?
FAT FREDDY. Just say it. *(With restraint.)* Say, "I love you, Poppa" even if you don't mean it. *(Pause.)* Please. *(Pause.)* Final request from a dying man. *(Pause.)* You want me to change my will?
DIANE. I love you, Poppa.
FAT FREDDY. *(Pause. Smiles.)* I love you, too, angel face. *(Starts to move toward her, then halts until a spasm of pain passes.)* Don't go to your house... come home and stay the

night... for old times' sake?... father and daughter. We'll play some cribbage.

DIANE. You can play cribbage with Celia.

FAT FREDDY. She's ugly.

DIANE. So are you.

FAT FREDDY. You're a bitch.

DIANE. Go to hell.

(FAT FREDDY pulls out the gun, points it at her. She gasps, backing up. Then he fires it away from her, into the floor.)

FAT FREDDY. *(Laughs.)* Scared ya, huh? *(Laughs more.)* Right... bullets! Remember what I always told you. Never trust anybody, not even your own. *(Pause.)* After you, angel face.

(DIANE backs up to the door, opens it, and backs out. FAT FREDDY follows, closing the door after him.)

(LIGHTS FADE)

(Music.)

Scene 3

(Two days later, late afternoon. As lights rise: JEANNIE is alone onstage. She is pacing, mumbling to herself. She stops, takes a drink of coffee, then continues to mumble. FAT FREDDY enters. She gasps. Silence.)

FAT FREDDY. Oh, Jeannie...

JEANNIE. You're disappointed.

FAT FREDDY. Jeannie, Jeannie, Jeannie. Oh, Jeannie...

JEANNIE. You're not going to... hurt me or anything.

FAT FREDDY. Why would I hurt you? What do you think I am?

JEANNIE. How did you know I was here?

FAT FREDDY. The hotel in Reno. They said you checked in, they said you checked out. I put one and one together.

JEANNIE. Why are you here?

FAT FREDDY. To collect my money... and... and see how you're doin'.

JEANNIE. Here's the money. *(Gets the briefcase, brings it to him.)* It's all there... except what I used. I'm sorry you're disappointed. It was all very generous of you, Mr. Fat Freddy, but you were trying to wreck my marriage.

FAT FREDDY. No, no, no. No. No, I wasn't. I was trying to give you some happiness, but here you are depriving yourself. Where's Russ?

JEANNIE. I don't know. Don't you know?

FAT FREDDY. I just asked you, how the hell would I know. Probably out chasing after you.

JEANNIE. Really?

FAT FREDDY. I gotta sit down. I was at death's door... but God gave me another reprieve... right, God? ... *so*!... I gotta get goin' here with rearrangements. Ours didn't work out so well, sweetness. Gotta move onto another track, gotta—

JEANNIE. You don't hate me.

FAT FREDDY. How could I hate you... a little pissed off maybe...

JEANNIE. *(Helps him out of his overcoat and takes his*

hat.) You really do like me.

FAT FREDDY. 'Course I like you.

JEANNIE. I'm glad. Because I like you, too... for some strange reason.

FAT FREDDY. Nothin' strange about it... I'm likeable.

(FAT FREDDY sits.)

JEANNIE. In a way I'm grateful to you. In the last two days I've made so many discoveries.

FAT FREDDY. Discoveries? Like...

JEANNIE. Oh, no, not like Madame Curie or Thomas Edison... not that kind, not like that. Personal discoveries.

FAT FREDDY. I've been eatin' too much crap... my stomach's wobbly. And I've swallowed so many pills, I'm all out of whack.

JEANNIE. *(Overlapping.)* Mr. Fat Freddy, I do think you meant well for me... in a twisted kind of way. I feel, in all fairness, that I should explain what happened to me.

FAT FREDDY. And this cold... I can't shake it.

JEANNIE. *(Overlapping.)* No, I should. It's important.

FAT FREDDY. *(Overlapping.)* I'll probably get pneumonia—That'll do me in before they cut me open again and do me in anyway.

(Blows his nose.)

JEANNIE. If I explain it to you it'll make it easier for me to explain it to Russ. *(RUSS enters. Pause.)* I'm back.

RUSS. I see.

FAT FREDDY. I'm back, too.

RUSS. Are you all right?

JEANNIE. I'm fine.

RUSS. Where have you been?—I went to Boston, I couldn't get a flight out so I drove to New York, to get a flight from La Guardia—

JEANNIE. You were coming after me?

RUSS. Yes... but I had to turn back because of the snowstorm.

JEANNIE. You were coming after me.

RUSS. Then I called your father and he—

JEANNIE. You and Dad *talked*?

RUSS. We were both concerned. He told me you'd left the hotel in Reno... we didn't know where you were.

JEANNIE. I'm here, I'm back, you see me. Oh, Russ... Russ, I want to explain it to you, I do. I'll begin at the beginning. I was just telling Mr. Fat Freddy—

RUSS. *(To FAT FREDDY.)* Why are you back in my house?

FAT FREDDY. You should charge me rent, huh?

RUSS. I-want-you-out-of-here.

JEANNIE. Russ, he came to get his money, he came—Russ, please. I want Mr. Fat Freddy to hear, too. He's entitled. It's important to me. Let me tell my story.

FAT FREDDY. Let her tell her story.

RUSS. Go ahead, go ahead.

(RUSS removes his overcoat.)

FAT FREDDY. Go ahead, Jeannie.

JEANNIE. Thank you. I'll begin at the beginning. I was hurt. *(Pause.)* You hurt me. Yes... yes, it was my father's suggestion... to remove the furniture. He said I shouldn't let you get away with murder. Then Mr. Fat Freddy caught me... when I was... an unguarded moment... and offered me all that money. Why did I accept?

RUSS. You were hurt.

JEANNIE. Yes, I was hurt... and Mr. Fat Freddy is very persuasive.

FAT FREDDY. Not persuasive enough.

RUSS. Let her finish.

JEANNIE. I'm just beginning. Anyway... I didn't call my father, it was my decision to go to Reno. I was... like in a trance! I went home and packed and left Dad and Mom a note, too... me!... went!... and the next thing I know I'm being driven to Hillsgrove Airport and I get into a very small plane and up we went—I loved it!—and landed in no time at La Guardia Airport just outside New York City, and the next thing I know I'm in another plane, a big one now—Oh, I *loved* it!—and having some champagne, *yes,* two glasses and then we landed in Chicago, and then right away flew off to Reno and—

RUSS. And you—

JEANNIE. Yes, I loved it!—And we landed in Reno... Nevada... in the middle of the night, and the next thing I know I'm being driven to a hotel and Mr. Fat Freddy said he'd made all the arrangements—

FAT FREDDY. I had—

JEANNIE. He had, and the next thing I know I'm in this elegant room... no, not a room, a *suite*, Russ... with red velvet curtains... and this huge, huge bouquet of yellow roses, not fake, real... for me! I felt enchanted!... and the next thing I know this old fraidy cat goes right to sleep... isn't that amazing? Please don't say anything, Russ. It's not easy to get through this—Thank you. And the next thing I know I've slept until ten the next morning! I hurried into the bathroom... oh, Russ, it was gigantic, and everything on the marble sink was wrapped up like a present... the soap, the shower cap, the little shampoo, the *teeniest* little sewing kit... ohhh, I felt like Cinderella!

FAT FREDDY. I need a pain killer.

(FAT FREDDY gets a pill from his pocket.)

JEANNIE. I'll get you some water.

(JEANNIE exits.)

FAT FREDDY. Maybe two.

JEANNIE. *(From offstage.)* I got under this glorious shower and washed my troubles away, and then, after I got dressed, downstairs in the stained glass dining room—Tiffany lamps, too... freshly squeezed orange in the tallest glass, nice sprigs of parsley on the poached eggs, everything so perfect and *expensive,* but did I care? No. And the next thing I know the friendly lady behind the front desk hands me an envelope about a courthouse appointment and further instructions because the next thing I know I was on the elevator going up again... *(Returning.)*... and that's when everything began to change because of Lisa.

FAT FREDDY. This is longer than Lolli the Elf.

RUSS. Lolli the Elf?

FAT FREDDY. Don't ask.

RUSS. *(Pause.)* I'm confused. I don't know where the hell I am. *(FAT FREDDY grunts.)* You're no help.

(JEANNIE hands FAT FREDDY the water.)

FAT FREDDY. Thanks.

(FAT FREDDY takes pill.)

RUSS. Who's Lisa?

JEANNIE. Well, Lisa couldn't tell me her name at first because she was sobbing so... and the elevator operator let us off on the seventh floor... same as mine. I tried to steady her, but she just stumbled forward and plopped down on the thick beige carpet. And the next thing I know—It seemed so natural—I sat *down* on the beige carpet beside her. She told me she'd been there, in Reno, for almost six weeks and she was in misery and revealed to me that her husband had had an affair with his secretary, and—please don't interrupt me now, Russ, please, this is hard—*and* that's when I told her about you with Diane the slut—I'm sorry, Mr. Fat Freddy, but truth is truth—and then this maid came out of the elevator with a vacuum and she just gawked at us, and the strangest thing happened. I wasn't embarrassed sitting there on the beige carpet comforting Lisa... no... and you know me... so many silly things bother me. *(RUSS nods.)* The maid, very snotty, asked us to move because she had to vacuum, and I said—You won't believe this, Russ—I *said*: "You can vacuum after we get up and not before." Well, that woman looked at me with daggers, but she went to the other end of the hallway and plugged in. I was so proud of myself.

RUSS. Good for you.

(FAT FREDDY blows his nose.)

JEANNIE. Lisa said her father had persuaded her to go to Reno for her divorce, and then I told her about my father punching you and you punching him and my brother punching you and me cracking you with the flashlight and then I said—Oh, I surprised myself again—I said: "I guess you have to change loyalties once you marry." *(Again FAT FREDDY blows his nose.)* Shhh-sh-sh. I made my decision right there on the beige carpet, and Lisa said she was going home to fight for her husband, too, and we got up off the carpet and went downstairs and made our reservations and the next thing I know I'm *back* in the air—Oh, I love flying! Lisa and I had to wait in Chicago for hours because of the snowstorm there and finally—Lisa begged me to go along to give her courage—we got to New York City and I went with her to the Empire State Building. Her husband's office was on the twentieth floor and up we went and in we went and she slapped his secretary. She did it so fast she didn't realize that it was a substitute secretary, not his regular one who had been his you-know-what. Well, the commotion got him out of his inner office and when he saw Lisa his eyes lit up and she rushed into his arms and they hugged and kissed and cried and she introduced me and then I left. I was in such a hurry to come back and make up with you that I forgot to throw up on the train.

FAT FREDDY. Trains useta make her throw up.

JEANNIE. Oh, I wanted to call and tell you I was coming home, but I didn't, I was afraid *she* might be here, and I thought:

If she's in this house when I get home I'll fight her... No offense, Mr. Fat Freddy... I'll get her out of my house—our house... and you and I will forgive each other and hold each other and... you say something, I'm speechless. *(Pause.)* Say something, Russ.

FAT FREDDY. Go ahead, don't hold back on account of me.

RUSS. *(Rises. To FAT FREDDY, restrained.)* I want you to take your money and leave.

FAT FREDDY. Russ... Russ, you're lookin' at a man whose demise is near. Be friendly, have a little compassion... and right now... I gotta go to the bathroom. *(Grunts. As he rises, JEANNIE moves to assist him.)* Thanks, thanks, but I can do it. *(And he's up.)* I know the way. When I come back we'll discuss all this, get it all straightened out...

RUSS. Discuss what?

FAT FREDDY. ... get it all rearranged...

(FAT FREDDY exits.)

RUSS. When I come home, night or day, day or night... he's here. I'm sick of that man in my house. He's a goddamned invader.

JEANNIE. *(Half a whisper.)* Are you glad I'm back?

RUSS. What do you think?

JEANNIE. *(Shaken, drained.)* I'm not sure. *(The tears come.)* I love you so much... I don't know how to say it... *(Pause.)* I love you, Russ.

RUSS. I love you, too, honey.

(RUSS moves to JEANNIE and takes her in his arms. They kiss.)

JEANNIE. Oh, you feel so good.

RUSS. You, too.

JEANNIE. I don't want to fight anymore.

RUSS. Me either. But we have to talk, Jeannie.

JEANNIE. I know. A marriage has to have compromises... to make it work. I said that ... to Lisa.

RUSS. Lisa?

JEANNIE. In the hotel hallway... on the plane back... I'm not sure where or which... *(Still in his arms. With warmth.)* Oh, I wish Mr. Fat Freddy weren't here now.

RUSS. *(Chuckles.)* I've got to get that man out of my house and out of my life.

JEANNIE. And you have to get his daughter out of your life, too.

RUSS. That's... what we have to talk about. I'm a... I'm a... I'm up in the air.

JEANNIE. What does that mean?

(The door flies open. DIANE enters.)

DIANE. *(Pause.)* You've been avoiding me.

RUSS. Yeah.

DIANE. Because she's back?

JEANNIE. *(Defiant.)* I'm back.

DIANE. When did she get back?

JEANNIE. About an hour ago. I still love him. Russ.

DIANE. I know who you're talking about.

JEANNIE. I realized... out there in Reno.

DIANE. I guess so. You're back.

JEANNIE. Yes, I'm back. For good.

RUSS. *(As DIANE starts to take off her coat.)* Keep it on, Diane. This is a private discussion.

DIANE. No, it isn't. I have to know where I stand. *She* wants it settled, *I* want it settled.

RUSS. *I've* got to get it settled.

DIANE. Just because the drip walks back into this house—

JEANNIE. *(Overlapping.)* Did she call me a drip?

DIANE. Look at you. All puffed up... with your battered face... wedged between two women. Look at him. He loves it... don't you. You do.

RUSS. I want my life simple!

DIANE. Ha!

RUSS. I can have that with Jeannie. I'd never have a simple life with you.

DIANE. We'd just fuck more.

JEANNIE. *(Explosively.)* I am not a *drip*! I demand that you apologize to me.

DIANE. You demand that I—

JEANNIE. Yes!

DIANE. And if I don't?

RUSS. Just apologize, Diane.

DIANE. I apologize.

JEANNIE. Thank you.

(DIANE takes off her coat, flings it aside, sits.)

RUSS. Are you going to be reasonable, or do I—

DIANE. Don't threaten me.

JEANNIE. I'm going to jump in here now. I have my life to live and life goes on, I need to know where I stand.

DIANE. You see? It's *not* settled.

JEANNIE. I'm back... to try again... together. Us.

RUSS. Will you just go, Diane.

DIANE. You can't live without me.

JEANNIE. I'll bring all the furniture back. Will you forgive me?

RUSS. Jeannie, there's nothing to forgive. I'm the one—

DIANE. She ran out on you!

RUSS. No. Your father instigated the whole—

DIANE. *(Weakening.)* Why are you doing this?

RUSS. I don't want to be owned by anybody.

DIANE. Who could own you?

RUSS. *(Bringing her her coat. Almost pleading.)* Will you get out of here? And take—

DIANE. You keep throwing me out of your house.

RUSS. *(Attempting lightness.)* Don't take it personally.

JEANNIE. Why do I feel like I'm not in this room?

DIANE. I *do* take it personally... *(Suddenly bursts into tears.)* Damn you. This is so stupid. I hate to cry. Damn it.

RUSS. *(Shaken.)* Oh, Diane... *(Kneels.)* Oh, baby, I don't want to—

JEANNIE. Did you call her *baby*? —You did!

RUSS.	DIANE.
I did?	What were you saying, baby?

JEANNIE. Something isn't right here.

RUSS. Wait a minute.

(RUSS rises.)

DIANE. What, baby?

JEANNIE. If you call me honey, you *cannot* call her—

DIANE. Baby, talk to—

RUSS. Wait a minute, hold it, both of you!

FAT FREDDY. *(From the bedroom doorway. To DIANE.)* Where did you come from?

DIANE. *(Rising.)* What are you... ? You're supposed to be home in bed. Doctor Russo gave strict orders—You were practically—

FAT FREDDY. Don't give me that *death's door* crap. I have a—

DIANE. I'm not talking to you. He tried to kill me.

FAT FREDDY. I did not, I just fired the gun. She exaggerates.

DIANE. You could've killed—

FAT FREDDY. Blame it on the pills.

DIANE. I'm not talking to you—I'm not talking to him. What are you doing here?

FAT FREDDY.	RUSS.
What are *you* doin' here?	He was here when—

JEANNIE. He came to get his money... and to see how I was.

DIANE. He did what?

JEANNIE. He likes me.

FAT FREDDY. I do.

RUSS. Don't sit, Fat Freddy. You're leaving. And take your daughter and you money with you.

FAT FREDDY. *(Sits.)* No, no, no, no, no, no. No. No, I'm here for a purpose... I didn't know. Please I was in there, sittin' on the throne, and I asked God to guide me—I did, Diane—I may have neglected God in the past, but it's never too late to get reacquainted. I did. I have. I gotta say he talked to me in there, in the bathroom. I had a vision, I swear to God, like a miracle!... it's true, angel face. When I came out of the bathroom I heard three voices, the three of you jabbering out here... and you know what I heard above the noise? I heard harmony.

DIANE. Don't' you dare sing *Alexander's Ragtime Band—*

FAT FREDDY. Shut up. Sit down. You, too, Russ. And Jeannie, you please sit... go on... no, no, let Russ sit in the middle between the two of you.

(Only JEANNIE sits in a theatre chair.)

RUSS. Goddamnit, enough is enough!

FAT FREDDY. Russ. You can't deny what happened to me in your bathroom. God works in mysterious ways, his wonders to perform.

DIANE. Oh, God.

(DIANE sits.)

FAT FREDDY. Exactly. So give a dying man a little respect, a little attention. Is that so much to ask?

JEANNIE. Russ, come sit. It's not much of a request from a... from a...

FAT FREDDY. A dying man, you can say it, I just said it. I'm getting fearless.

DIANE. *(Rising. Concerned.)* How many pills have you taken to—

FAT FREDDY. Like I'm always sayin'... when you're on one track too long, sometimes ya gotta switch directions fast— Rearrangements!

DIANE. *(Almost simultaneously.)* Rearrangements. *(Sits again.)* Oh, humor him, Russ. Come—

JEANNIE. Sit, honey. I'm sitting, she's sitting. It's the least we—

FAT FREDDY. Right, Jeannie. *Now.* I figure my demise... has been postponed so I can do God's will, bring some happiness to you three... C'mon, Russ, go along with me for a minute or two. C'mon, don't grunt, sit.

RUSS. *(Pause.)* Two minutes, that's it.

(RUSS sits. Now the three are in the theatre chairs.)

FAT FREDDY. Terrific!... Oh, yeah, between the two beauties... perfect! Now. Take their hands, Russ... c'mon, a minor request... c'mon, take Diane's hand... Jeannie's hand... yeah, yeah... good! Feel the electricity... runnin' through the three of ya? They say two's company, three's a crowd. Don't let anybody kid ya. The best things in life are three... yeah, I'm tellin' ya. Oh, I'm not sayin' what's right, what's wrong—

(FAT FREDDY rises.)

DIANE. What are you saying, Poppa dear?

FAT FREDDY. I'm sayin'—if you'd just listen for once—I'm sayin' people are entitled to happiness, and if you haveta bend the rules a little... well, what the hell, that's—

RUSS.	JEANNIE.
Bend the rules?	I'm not sure—

FAT FREDDY. Hold tight, Russ, I beg you, hold those hands. Feel the electricity?—I see it in you faces. Feel the love?

DIANE. Oh, for the love of—

FAT FREDDY. That's it, angel face, you're right... For the love of.

RUSS. One minute left.

FAT FREDDY. Don't you see? This is a time of discovery. Hold tight, Russ, it's true. *Now.* Jeannie went and made personal discoveries about herself... one big one! She got courage... you did, sweetness... and you put love before money... that's a discovery.

DIANE. Something you'd never understand, big shot.

FAT FREDDY. And you, angel face, even with your smart mouth, you discovered your need for love is stronger than your need for money, too... and sometimes even *you* gotta bend a little. And Russ here... oh, yeah... tryin' to find your way, yeah... and you have a *dilemma* and a discovery. Lovin' two women at the same time, *discovery... God bestowed upon you the gift of love*! Right under your nose all the time. *Now.* Clear up your dilemma, accept the discovery, and rearrange, Russ. She loves you, you love her, you love her, she loves you. Ya hear what I'm sayin'?

DIANE. I hear what you're saying. Half a loaf of fresh bread is sometimes better than a whole loaf of stale.

JEANNIE. What?

DIANE. And *I* say: Bullshit.

(DIANE rises.)

FAT FREDDY. *(Pulling out a gun.)* Shut up and sit down!

(And RUSS and JEANNIE are up.)

JEANNIE.
Oh, Mr. Fat Freddy—

RUSS.
Put that gun away.

DIANE. Are you nuts?

FAT FREDDY. Yeah, yeah, I'm nuts. *Now sit...* and HOLD THOSE GODDAMN HANDS!

(JEANNIE and DIANE sit.)

JEANNIE.	RUSS.
That's dangerous, Mr. Fat Freddy... Shouldn't—	Put...it... down.

DIANE. Just give it to me and let me put you out of your misery.

FAT FREDDY. Shut up! All of you! I have this fucking vision and I want to lead you three into fucking happiness and you give me fucking aggravation! *(To RUSS.) I said sit.*

RUSS. Give me the gun.

FAT FREDDY. You stay back or I'll—

RUSS. No you won't.

(RUSS moves fast, taking the gun from him.)

DIANE. *(Almost simultaneously.)* Don't hurt him.

RUSS. What the hell do you think you're doing?

FAT FREDDY. Did you see that? Brave, huh? *(As RUSS pockets the gun.)* He didn't fear for his life, did he. Somebody threatened him, he was ready, *defending* both of you. I bet you don't know where it comes from?

RUSS. *(With humor.)* Don't tell me. *(Again sits between the two women.)* It comes from the *electricity.*

(Grabs up their hands, then lets the hands go.)

FAT FREDDY. It's not a joke, Russ.

DIANE. Your two minutes are up, Poppa.

FAT FREDDY. No, they're not... you know they're not. Don't fight it, Russ. *(With his hands makes RUSS again take the women's hands.)* You're an innovator, that's what you are, so you gotta innovate. Look at the three of you sittin' there... together... like you're sittin' in the theatre watchin' the screen... and most of the time in the movies there's a happy ending, right? And that's what you three can have in life—be happy!—*if* you just listen to Fat Freddy—My vision! My good deed... before my demise. Then straight to heaven I go. *(Pause.)* 'Scuse me, I'll be right back, I gotta go again. When I come back we'll get it worked out. *(Starts off, hesitates. Matter-of-fact.)* By the way, the money in the briefcase. Three ways. It's only fair.

(FAT FREDDY exits. Silence.)

JEANNIE. What was that about a loaf of bread?

DIANE. He's really gone nuts.

RUSS. Maybe... when all is said and done... we should consider what he had to say.

(DIANE and JEANNIE look at him.)

JEANNIE. Ohhhh.

(JEANNIE rises.)

DIANE. *(Rises.)* Uh huh.

(JEANNIE and DIANE exchange a glance, then look back at RUSS, then back to one another.)

JEANNIE. *(To DIANE.)* Would you like a cup of coffee?

DIANE. I'd love a cup of coffee.

JEANNIE. Then follow me.

(JEANNIE and DIANE exit into the kitchen. Silence.)

FAT FREDDY. *(Returning.)* Where are they?

RUSS. In the kitchen. Having coffee.

FAT FREDDY. Oh, oh.

RUSS. It ain't like the movies, Fat Freddy.

FAT FREDDY. *(Sitting.)* Russ. I really did have a vision in there.

RUSS. Sounded good to me. *(Pause. Rises.)* But I'm afraid...

FAT FREDDY. *(Sniffing.)* My cold's better. Now I can die happy.

RUSS. You'll never die.

(Laughter is heard from the kitchen.)

RUSS. What do you think they're talking about?

FAT FREDDY. What do you think? Rearrangements.

(More laughter from the kitchen. RUSS starts toward the kitchen.)

FAT FREDDY. Russ, don't go in there, don't—

RUSS. You really had me for a minute.

FAT FREDDY. You're supposed to innovate, not intervene! *(RUSS exits. Rising.)* Russ... *(Debates about following him. Sighs.)* Nobody has any imagination anymore. Right, God? *(Pause.)* Right!

(DIANE returns, immediately getting into her coat.)

FAT FREDDY. What happened in—

DIANE. Put on your coat and hat.

FAT FREDDY. I'm entitled to an explana—

DIANE. You're entitled to jello.

FAT FREDDY. You tell me what happened or—

DIANE. *I* had a vision.

FAT FREDDY. You did?! *(Laughs.)* You see. Like father, like daught—

DIANE. Let's go.

(DIANE picks up the briefcase.)

FAT FREDDY. I'll carry that.

DIANE. No, I'll carry it. Let's go.

FAT FREDDY. Don't be so bossy.

DIANE. After you, Poppa dear.

FAT FREDDY. That's better, angel face. You didn't tell me. What was your vision?

DIANE. Move.

FAT FREDDY. About the money in the briefcase, huh?

(DIANE manages to get FAT FREDDY out the door. Silence. RUSS returns. JEANNIE follows cautiously.)

JEANNIE. They've gone?

RUSS. Keep your fingers crossed. *(Pause.)* Can I interest you in a seat in the balcony?

(RUSS gestures toward the theatre chairs.)

JEANNIE. Depends on what's showing.

RUSS. It's called Russ and Jeannie live happily ever after... what do you say?

(RUSS reaches out his hand. JEANNIE hesitates and then takes his hand. They start toward the theatre chairs. The door flies open. DIANE returns.)

DIANE. My father's gun...

RUSS. Oh. *(Removes it from his pocket, hands it to her. As she starts toward the open front door.)* "Thank you." You're welcome.

(DIANE quickly turns, points the gun at them. JEANNIE gasps.)

DIANE. If you think this is the end... think again. *(Lowers the gun.)* Ciao.

(DIANE exits. RUSS puts a protective arm around JEANNIE as the lights fade.)

END OF PLAY

COSTUME PLOT

FAT FREDDY

Act I, Scene 2

Overcoat
Fedora
Dark Pinstripe Suit (w/vest)
Tie (w/diamond clip)
Shirt
Handkerchief
White Silk Scarf
Diamond Ring

Act II, Scene 1

Overcoat
Fedora
Gray Suit
Buttoned Sweater
Tie
Shirt
Handkerchief
White Silk Scarf

Act II, Scene 2

Same

Act II, Scene 3

Other Overcoat
Fedora
White Silk Scarf
Suit (same as Act 2, Sc.1.)

Buttoned Sweater
Tie
Shirt
Handkerchief

RUSS

Act I, Scene 1
Plaid wool shirt (Unbuttoned)
T-Shirt
Corduroy pants
Socks
Shoes

Act I, Scene 2
(Remove plaid shirt, put on pullover sweater)
(Add:)
Winter Jacket
Gloves
Scarf

Act I, Scene 3
T-shirt
Undershorts
Robe

Act II, Scene 2
Overcoat
Sweater
Pants
Shoes
Scarf

Gloves

Act II, Scene 3
Overcoat
Shirt
Tie (loosened)
Sweater vest (Buttons)
Socks
Shoes
Gloves
Scarf

DIANE

Act I, Scene 1
Skating outfit
—fitted jacket
—short skirt
—tights
—scarf
Earmuffs
High Heeled boot or heel
Pair of white skates (slung over shoulder)

Act I, Scene 3
Long winter coat
—wool, not fur
Dressy dress
High heels
Earrings
Head Scarf
Purse

Act II, Scene 2
Overcoat
Slacks
Turtleneck Sweater
White Silk Scarf
Heeled boot
Shoulder bag
Gloves

Act II, Scene 3
Overcoat
White Silk Scarf
Skirt
Blouse
Stockings
Shoes

JEANNIE

Act I, Scene 2
Bright winter jacket
Scarf
Headwear
Wool Gloves
Skirt
Sweater
High socks
Loafers (Or boots)
Shoulder bag

<u>Act II, Scene 1</u>

Skirt
Blouse
Shoes
socks
Bright Winter Jacket
Scarf
Shoulder Bag

<u>Act II, Scene 3</u>

Dress
Shoes
Stockings

FURNITURE PLOT

Act I

Fireplace
3 attached theatre chairs
Large braided oval rug
Coffee table
Sofa with four pillows and throw
Ottoman
Armchair with one pillow
Handmade dining table (off kitchen)
3 chairs (not quite matching table)
Large tapestry rug
Large armchair
Ottoman/bench
Floor lamp
2 bookcases/benches
Telephone table
Straight backed chair
Coat Rack (near front door)

Act II

During intermission some furniture is removed
(See Property list.)

PROPERTY LIST

Act I, Scene 1

PRESET:

- Fireplace mantle
  - Vase
  - Photo of Russ and Jeannie
  - Ashtray
  - Candle holder (brass)
  - A few small knick knacks
  - Camel unfiltered cigarettes (half pack)
  - Lighter
- Coffee Table
  - Tray
  - Magazines (*Life Holiday*)
  - Ashtray on doily
  - Book with bookmark
- Telephone table
  - Telephone (dial)
- 2 Bookcases/benches w/removable cushions
  - Books (of the period)
  - 2 Photograph albums
  - Phonograph recore albums (78's, LP's)
- Dining table w/ 3 chairs
  - Runner (for table)
  - Trivet
  - Ashtray
  - Lighter (Back up)
- Coat rack
  - Coat, 2 jackets, scarfs, a hat or two, etc.

PRESET — OFF Front door
White ice skates (Diane)
Aluminum foiled chocolate heart (Diane)
PRESET — OFF Kitchen area
Can of beer (Carling's Black Label - Russ)

Act I, Scene 2
SET - Onstage
By large armchair
Briefcase (Filled with $20 bills in bundles)
PRESET - Offstage Front door
Gun (Fat Freddy)
PRESET - OFF Kitchen area
2 cans of beer, Black Label (Russ)
Church key (Russ)
PRESET - OFF Bedroom area
Shoulder bag (Jeannie)

STRIKE: End of Act 1, Scene 3 (Intermission)
Beer cans
Diane's discarded shoes, coat, etc.
Russ' robe
Sofa
Ottoman
Coffee table
Large braided oval rug
3 Dining room chairs
Cushions on bookcase/benches (if used)

Act II, Scene 1

PRESET - Onstage

On floor by bedroom entrance

Small bed lamp

Large paper bag (w/towel items)

On chair

Shoulder bag (Jeannie's same bag as in Act I,Sc.2)

Bright winter jacket (Jeannie's same jacket as in Act I, Sc. 2)

PRESET - OFF Kitchen area

Toaster (Jeannie

PRESET - OFF Front door

Briefcase (Fat Freddy)

Gun (Fat Freddy) - (Fired in Act 2, Sc. 2)

Small prescription bottle of pills (Fat Freddy)

STRIKE: (End of Act II, Sc.1)

Briefcase

Shoulder bag

Bright winter jacket

Bed lamp

Large paper bag (w/towel items, toaster)

SET: For Act II, Scene 2

On Table

A Note. It reads: Russ, I had furnishings that belong to me, mostly, put in storage. I am on my way to Reno to get a divorce. I don't know what else to say. Sincerely, Jeannie.

SET - OFF Bedroom area
Fat Freddy's overcoat, hat, suit jacket (Diane)

PRESET - OFF kitchen area
Glass of water (Diane)

SET: For Act II, Scene 3
On table
Coffee cup and saucer
By table
Briefcase

PRESET - OFF Kitchen area
Glass of water (Jeannie)

PRESET - OFF Front door area
Gun (Fat Freddy)

SOUND
Instrumental music of the period used between scenes.

SET: Act II, Scene 2
Car starting and pulling away (while front door is open)

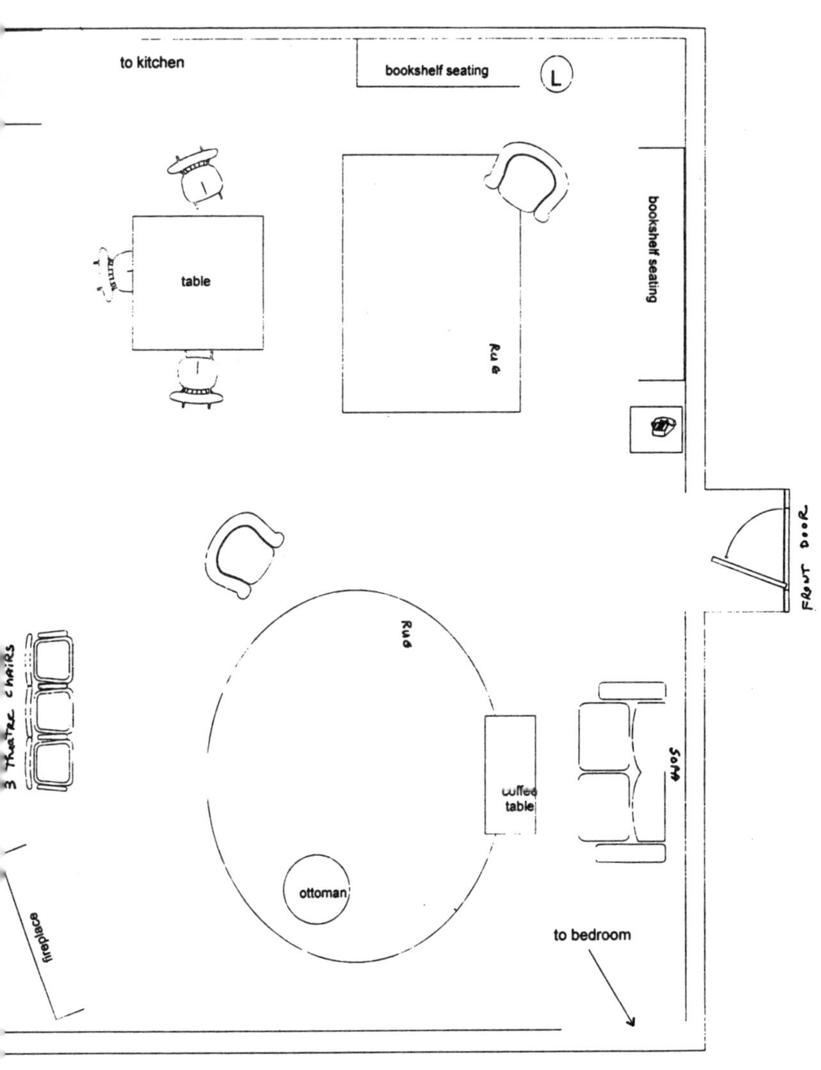

ND FAT FREDDY'S BLUES

ground plan version
1/4 inch = 1 foot

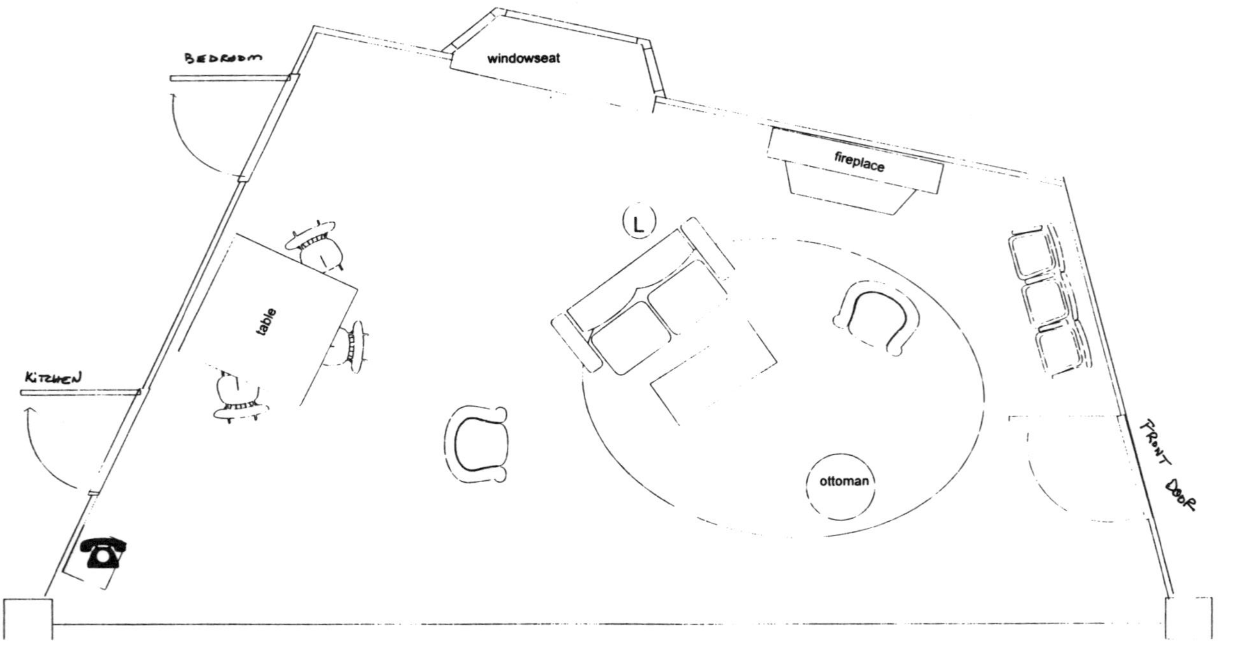

AND FAT FREDDY'S BLUES   Proscenium Ground Plan   1/4 in = 1 ft

Picasso at the Lapin Agile

STEVE MARTIN

"Very good fun."
NEW YORK TIMES
"Very funny ... [and] daring."
NEW YORK POST

This long-running Off-Broadway hit places Albert Einstein and Pablo Picasso in a Parisian cafe in 1904, just before the renowned scientist transformed physics and the celebrated painter set the world afire. In his first stage comedy, the popular actor and screenwriter plays fast and loose with fact, fame and fortune as these two geniuses interact with infectious dizziness. 7 m., 2 f. (#18962)

Arts & Leisure

STEVE TESICH

Written by the popular author of TOUCHING BOTTOM, ON THE OPEN ROAD, THE SPEED OF DARKNESS and other plays, this brilliantly caustic play is centered around a self-absorbed drama critic who judges theater and life by the same criteria, to absurd extremes. He is confronted by the bitter and alienated women who have suffered from his unyieldingly clinical detachment and his habit of judging their suffering by its dramatic effect on him. 1 m., 4 f. (#3866)

ROAD TO NIRVANA
by Arthur Kopit

Dark comedy

Advanced Groups

(2m., 2f. 2 exts.)Ex-movie mogul Al has invited his old pal Jerry, another ex-mogul, over for a visit, to do lunch, take a meeting, and so on. Jerry is pretty desperate to get back into the film business. He has been producing educational films the past few years, ever since Al fired him, after first screwing his wife, who then committed suicide. In other words, Jerry's life and career is basically in the toilet; still he comes to Al's house, enticed by a vague promise of re-entry into the intoxicating world of Hollywood deal-making. Al is also on the skids; but he has a hot property, and needs Jerry to co-produce it with him. It seems the world's hottest female rock star has written an autobiographical screenplay and is willing to star in it herself—if, that is, she can find a producer willing to meet her terms. Apparently, Al has already met these terms. He has slit his wrists to demonstrate his commitment to the project, and he wants Jerry to do the same. Jerry is, of course, very reluctant—particularly when he learns that the "screenplay" is, word-for-word, *Moby Dick*—except that Nirvana, the rock star, has substituted herself for Ahab and a huge penis for the great white whale! Ridiculous, you say? Of course—but that's Hollywood, the living, breathing, real-life theatre of the absurd. Jerry finally does cut his wrists, and undergoes other degrading acts to demonstrate his wish to be a part of the Big Deal. In the second act, we meet the whacked-out Nirvana—and we learn just what it is that Al needs Jerry to consummate the deal. Jerry is asked to prove his commitment *again:* Nirvana wants his balls. She already has Al's; but she wants more. And Jerry must *really, finally* decide just how much he wants to make the deal. "Mr. Kopit arouses audiences with his acerbity, his pitch-black humor and his sheer virulence."—N.Y. Times. "Careens madly from farce to fantasy and back again, and it makes for a consistently entertaining evening."—Louisville Courier-Journal. "A malicious and effective send-up of David Mamet's *Speed-the-Plow*, yet it has a vigor, and a vinegar, of its own."—Time Mag. "Gruffly announcing itself as scurrilous talk, it rapidly escalates into a dirty joke—funny enough to make you hoarse,.then into an outsize legend before, finally, rounding itself off as the equivalent of a modern morality play."—Boston Globe. **(#20134)**

CEMENTVILLE
by Jane Martin
Comedy
Little Theatre

(5m., 9f.) Int. The comic sensation of the 1991 Humana Festival at the famed Actors Theatre of Louisville, this wildly funny new play by the mysterious author of *Talking With* and *Vital Signs* is a brilliant portrayal of America's fascination with fantasy entertainment, "the growth industry of the 90's." We are in a run-down locker room in a seedy sports arena in the Armpit of the Universe, "Cementville, Tennessee," with the scurviest bunch of professional wrasslers you ever saw. This is decidedly a small-time operation—not the big time you see on TV. The promoter, Bigman, also appears in the show. He and his brother Eddie are the only men, though; for the main attraction(s) are the "ladies." There's Tiger, who comes with a big drinking problem and a small dog; Dani, who comes with a large chip on her shoulder against Bigman, who owes all the girls several weeks' pay; Lessa, an ex-Olympic shotputter with delusions that she is actually employed presently in athletics; and Netty, an overweight older woman who appears in the ring dressed in baggy pajamas, with her hair in curlers, as the character "Pajama Mama." There is the eager-beaver go-fer Nola, a teenager who dreams of someday entering the glamorous world of pro wrestling herself. And then, there are the Knockout Sisters, refugees from the Big Time but banned from it for heavy-duty abuse of pharmaceuticals as well as having gotten arrested *in flagrante delicto* with the Mayor of Los Angeles. They have just gotten out of the slammer; but their indefatigable manager, Mother Crocker ("Of the Auto-Repair Crockers") hopes to get them reinstated, if she can keep them off the white powder. Bigman has hired the Knockout Sisters as tonight's main attraction, and the fur really flies along with the sparks when the other women find out about the Knockout Sisters. Bigman has really got his hands full tonight. He's gotta get the girls to tear each other up in the ring, not the locker room; he's gotta deal with tough-as-nails Mother Crocker; he's gotta keep an arena full of tanked-up rubes from tearing up the joint—and he's gotta solve the mystery of who bit off his brother Eddie's dick last night. **(#5580)**

✓✓✓✓✓✓✓✓✓✓✓✓✓✓✓✓✓✓✓✓✓✓✓✓✓✓✓✓✓✓✓

OTHER PUBLICATIONS FOR YOUR INTEREST

COASTAL DISTURBANCES

(Little Theatre- Comedy)

by TINA HOWE

3 male, 4 female

This new Broadway hit from the author of *PAINTING CHURCHES, MUSEUM,* and *THE ART OF DINING* is quite daring and experimental, in that it is *not* cynical or alienated about love and romance. This is an ensemble play about four generations of vacationers on a Massachusetts beach which focuses on a budding romance between a hunk of a lifeguard and a kooky young photographer. Structured as a series of vignettes taking place over the course of the summer, the play looks at love from all sides now. "A modern play about love that is, for once, actually about love--as opposed to sexual, social or marital politics . . . it generously illuminates the intimate landscape between men and women." --NY Times. "Enchanting."--New Yorker. #5755

APPROACHING ZANZIBAR

(Advanced Groups—Comedy)

by TINA HOWE

2 male, 4 female, 3 children --Various Ints. and Exts.

This new play by the author of *Painting Churches, Coastal Disturbances, Museum,* and *The Art of Dining* is about the cross-country journey of the Blossom family--Wallace and Charlotte and their two kids Turner and Pony--out west to visit Charlotte's aunt Olivia Childs in Taos, New Mexico. Aunt Olivia, a renowned environmental artist who creates enormous "sculptures" of hundreds of kites, is dying of cancer, and Charlotte wants to see her one last time. The family camps out along the way, having various adventures and meeting other relatives and strangers, until, eventually, they arrive in Taos, where Olivia is fading in and out of reality--or is she? Little Pony Blossom persuades the old lady to stand up and jump up and down on the bed, and we are left with final entrancing image of Aunt Olivia and Pony bouncing on the bed like a trampoline. Has a miracle occurred? "What pervades the shadow is Miss Howe's originality and purity of her dramatic imagination."--The New Yorker. #3140